CODING
+MATH

Strengthen K–5 Math Skills With Computer Science

NICOL R. HOWARD AND KEITH E. HOWARD

International Society for Technology in Education

PORTLAND, OREGON • ARLINGTON, VIRGINIA

Coding + Math
Strengthen K-5 Math Skills with Computer Science
Nicol R. Howard, Keith E. Howard

© 2020 International Society for Technology in Education

Acquisitions Editor: *Valerie Witte*
Managing Editor: *Emily Reed*
Copy Editor: *Camille Cole*
Proofreader: *Angela B. Wade*
Indexer: *Wendy Allex*
Book Design and Production: *Jeff Puda*
Cover Design: *Edwin Ouellette*

Library of Congress Control Number: 2020933432

First Edition

ISBN: 9781564848253
Ebook version available.

Printed in the United States of America.

ISTE® is a registered trademark of the International Society for Technology in Education.

About ISTE

The International Society for Technology in Education (ISTE) is the premier non-profit organization serving educators and education leaders committed to empowering connected learners in a connected world. ISTE serves more than 100,000 education stakeholders throughout the world.

ISTE innovative offerings include the ISTE Conference & Expo, one of the biggest, most comprehensive ed tech events in the world, as well as the widely adopted ISTE Standards for learning, teaching, and leading in the digital age and a robust suite of professional learning resources, including webinars, online courses, consulting services for schools and districts, books, and peer-reviewed journals and publications. Visit iste.org to learn more.

Join our community of passionate educators!

ISTE members get free year-round professional development opportunities and discounts on ISTE resources and conference registration. Membership also connects you to a network of educators who can instantly help with advice and best practices.

Join or renew your ISTE membership today!

Visit iste.org/membership or call 800.336.5191.

Related ISTE Titles

Transform Your K-5 Math Class: Digital Age Tools to Spark Learning
by Amanda Thomas

Transform Your 6-12 Math Class: Digital Age Tools to Spark Learning
by Amanda Thomas

Rev Up Robotics: Real-World Computational Thinking in the K-8 Classroom
by Jorge Valenzuela

To see all books available from ISTE, please visit **iste.org/resources**.

About the Authors

 **Nicol R. Howard, PhD,** is an assistant professor in the School of Education at the University of Redlands. She has served as cochair for the ISTE Digital Equity Network, chair of the American Education Research Association's Technology, Instruction, Cognition, and Learning SIG, and cochair for the California Council on Teacher Education (CCTE) Technology SIG. Her research foci are teacher education, STEM and computer science opportunities for students of color, and equitable uses of technology in K–16 classrooms. Her writing has appeared in ISTE publications, the Corwin Connected Educators Series, and various educational journals. She is also the cofounder and coeditor of the *Journal of Computer Science Integration.*

 **Keith E. Howard, PhD,** is an associate professor in the Attallah College of Educational Studies at Chapman University. He obtained his PhD in Educational Psychology and Technology from the University of Southern California. He is cofounder and coeditor of the *Journal of Computer Science Integration.* He has served as co-program chair for the Teacher Education Innovation and Policy Section of the American Educational Research Association's Division K (Teaching and Teacher Education), board member for the California Council on Teacher Education (CCTE), as well as a cochair for the CCTE Technology SIG. He is a former secondary computer science and mathematics teacher for the Los Angeles Unified School District. His research foci include computer science in K–12 education, equity in K–12 STEM education, and teacher education.

Contributors

Kamau is a nine-year-old fourth-grader. He enjoys both mathematics and computer science.

Megan Brannon is a student in the Curriculum and Instruction/Educational Technology doctoral program at Kent State University. She has more than ten years of experience in K–12 education, working as both a teacher and technology integration specialist for her school district.

Ari Flewelling is a K–12 education strategist with CDW-G, from Southern California. She specializes in partnering with districts to help them plan and reach their strategic goals for 21st-century teaching. She is a former K–12 staff development specialist for technology and innovation.

Cory Gleasman, PhD, is an assistant professor of computer science in the Department of Curriculum and Instruction at Tennessee Technological University.

Veronica Godinez is a former teacher and current administrator with a passion for computer science. She serves on the board for Computer Using Educators (CUE).

Elena Novak, PhD, is an associate professor of educational technology at Kent State University. She earned her PhD in Instructional Systems and Learning Technologies from Florida State University. Elena Novak's research aims to advance STEM learning using technologies.

Shana V. White is a veteran educator who just finished her fourteenth year in education, serving in both public and private schools as a health/physical education teacher in metro Atlanta. She has also served as an instructional technology coordinator in Gwinnett County Public Schools.

Acknowledgments

This book has been published with the contribution of a mini grant from the School of Education, University of Redlands.

Dedication

To my husband, Keith, for his forever love, kindness, and support.
To our children for keeping us young and inspired to do this work.

Nicol R. Howard

Thank you to my wife, Nicol, for your love and support.
Thank you to our children for your kind spirits and endless pursuit of intellect.
Thank you to my parents, Herman and Willimeaner, for your protection
and support throughout life's many challenges.

Keith E. Howard

Contents

3

Data Dialogue

4

Operations and Loops

5

Events and Conditionals

6

Diving Deeper into CS and Math Connections

Final Thoughts

Introduction

Science, technology, engineering, and mathematics (STEM) innovations continue to be important factors in the growth and development of economies around the world. STEM initiatives, including an increase in the implementation of a range of computer science (CS) programs in K–5 classrooms, such as Code.org, Code Club, CoderDojo, and Learn to Code, are on the rise. Under these initiatives, CS education often includes what is considered basic coding, computer programming, and computational thinking. For this reason, the term coding is used more frequently in K–5 classrooms to refer to computer-science- and computer-programming-related activities. However, in this book the term coding is used to identify the basic entry into CS, while the term computer science (CS) is used to encompass that deeper level of thinking desired from K–5 students in a rapidly evolving technological society. The line between the two is often blurred, but understanding the baseline definition and practices of both is essential for the appropriate integration of CS in mathematics.

Researchers have suggested that students benefit from motivational factors related to coding; however, little is known about the potential impact of programming and computational thinking on elementary-aged students' achievement (Howard, 2018). Regardless, there is an emerging consensus about the importance of teaching coding in elementary grades. We are witnessing international efforts to expand coding programs to include more students. Expanding access to coding potentially means an earlier introduction to the deeper lessons taught through CS and programming into elementary classrooms. Such an expansion helps to increase the quality and quantity of students in the STEM pipeline (Tran, 2018). Furthermore, the current trajectory remains as an engaged digital era in which more CS, programming, and software engineering mindsets will be in demand; therefore, there is an increased need for K–5 educators to prepare to integrate CS into their current instruction with fidelity. In doing so, we recognize that there are obvious benefits to selecting visual-based over text-based programming as an ideal entry point to CS for elementary grade levels (Figure 0.1).

```
                    #include <iostream>
                    using namespace std;

                    int main() {
VS.                     cout << "Hello world!" << endl;
                        return 0;
                    }
```

Figure 0.1 *Hello World*: program comparison of a visual-based vs. text-based programming language (photo credit: Emily de la Pena).

According to de la Pena (2017), visual-based programming is more readable, easier to use with limited technical knowledge, and requires less typing than text-based programming. We encourage the approach of using visual-based programming in elementary settings, and we also support the idea of providing a high ceiling to create opportunities for students to explore further. Additionally, we recognize that leveraging CS interest and engagement to teach mathematics offers young learners an opportunity to make real-world connections between CS and math, while potentially increasing mathematics achievement gains. For example, elementary students may be asked in an integrated CS and math lesson to write code to construct shapes in order to evaluate their geometric reasoning. Instead of the CS activity occurring as a separate activity, the elementary students are immersed in the CS experience through a core content area. The CS and math lesson would engage students, but more importantly, educators would have an opportunity to introduce integrated lessons aligned to standards that prepare elementary students for future classes.

What's in This Book?

Throughout subsequent chapters, we will juxtapose visual-based and text-based activities through research-based project examples to demonstrate how to differentiate instruction in order to ensure young learners are exposed to both forms of programming before reaching secondary grade levels. The projects will demonstrate alignment with Common Core Mathematics Principles and Standards, CSTA K–12 Standards, and the K–12 Computer Science Framework. At the same time, persistent and substantial learning differentials call for additional strategies to fill the gap between the adoption of standards and the enactment of practices, programs, and actions required for the successful implementation of those standards (NCTM,

2014). Therefore, we will also outline the four practices in Brennan and Resnick's Computational Thinking Framework and the importance of seeking "Mission Clarity" when choosing the right curriculum path for students.

With this in mind, chapters in this book will include the following:

- Current research related to the inclusion of CS in K–5 classrooms

- Recommendations on how to incorporate CS to support strengthening math skills

- Practical programming examples that encourage "Getting Out the Blocks"

- Mission Clarity reminders to further support the decision-making process for CS integration in your own classroom

Throughout the book, you will see references to the ISTE Computer Science Standards for Educators. The ISTE Standards are a framework designed to support CS educators with the purposeful integration of technology. Although the CS Standards are not the primary focus of this book, it is imperative that consideration be given to the call for continued professional learning and the inclusion of each strand when designing projects for students.

Who Is This Book For?

This book is designed to reflect the contributions of faculty and K–12 leaders seeking to ensure that our approaches to incorporating coding in K–5 classrooms are informed by a clear understanding of its purpose. In addition to enhancing learning across different subject areas, coding can be the foundation for more in-depth CS studies later in the K–12 continuum, as well as for professional pursuit of CS-related careers. Some CS initiatives are explicitly designed to facilitate self-expression and develop social support channels, while others take the long view of providing conceptual and skill-based knowledge that can make the burgeoning field of CS more accessible to students underrepresented in the field. We seek to provide insight, research, and recommendations to assist educators in making curriculum-approach decisions that are in the best interests of their students.

Best,

Nicol and Keith

Overview of Computer Science in K–5 Mathematics

This chapter gives an overview of computer science in elementary settings, including information on how computing was first taught, how it has evolved to what we see today, and what we can expect to see in coming years.

Also included in this chapter:

- **Research on the effectiveness of block coding**
- **Exploration of computational thinking concepts and practices**
- **Feature: "Involving Parents in Coding Success" by Veronica Godinez**
- **Resources to get started**

Some form of computer science in elementary school settings has become more of an expectation for all students than an innovative rendezvous for privileged and fortunate school districts and schools. A brief history of computing's origins in the elementary classroom will contextualize the kinds of computing prevalent in K–5 settings today and provide some insights into the major influences on the thinking that has shaped our instructional approaches to learning with computers. As personal computers first started to gain a foothold in schools in the late 1970s and early 1980s, Seymour Papert's Logo programming language, written for teaching children to program via activities with a digital or robotic turtle, was a central component in harnessing the power of computers to help young children develop mathematical ideas and understanding. Papert, a South African born mathematician, computer scientist, and a protégé of Jean Piaget, was inspired by the role that his love of gears as a young child played in his own subsequent love of abstract ideas in mathematics. He relied heavily on Piaget's cognitive view of learning in natural settings without actually being *taught*, though he extended the concept to include affective influences that impact learning as well (Papert, 1980; 1993).

Papert believed that CS, through computer programming, could enable young children to acquire important mathematical ideas unencumbered by the math-phobic culture he saw as prevalent in the U.S. and Europe. Just as his connection to physical gears gave him an "object to think with," he believed his Turtle Geometry, using a specific language called Turtle Talk, provided students an object with which to think through geometric concepts. Although the early years witnessed millions of students learning to program using LOGO or Basic (another programming language designed to teach the basic tenets of programming to beginners), the use of computers in school to teach programming waned in subsequent years. This has been attributed to difficult programming languages (at that time) and activities that lacked meaningful connection to students, lives (Resnick et al., 2009). Papert lamented the prominent use of computers in school to "program the children" rather than allowing the children to "program the computer" (Papert, 1993) and viewed traditional classroom instruction as an inefficient learning environment. He criticized the academics who began to conduct experiments to determine whether Logo could, in and of itself, cause changes in children's thinking. He viewed Logo more as a tool that would make such changes possible. He opined that computers might allow us to create alternative learning spaces outside the classroom wherein children could learn without organized instruction. He acknowledged that his views implied that schools as we knew them might have no place in the future, giving way to a setting more conducive to a less formalized instructional approach (p. 9).

Block Coding: Meaningful Programming or Just Scratching the Surface?

Computer science and programming have seen resurgence in K–5 classrooms in recent years thanks, in large part, to Papert's colleagues at the MIT Media Lab he helped to create. In 2007, they launched the Scratch website aimed at helping kids from ages eight to sixteen learn to code, and later collaborated on the creation of the Scratch Jr. computer application designed as a similar, but less complex, version accessible to five-to-seven-year-olds. By 2009, users around the world were uploading over 1,500 new projects daily (Resnick et al., 2009). As of 2019, there have been over 44 million projects shared on the site (scratch.mit.edu/statistics), 43% of which are from users in the United States. Scratch tops the list of visual block programming languages based on search engine results (Zhang & Nouri, 2019). A cursory look at the platform reveals that it parallels the ideas behind Papert's Turtle project. It started with a specialized child-friendly language (initially Squeak, but later Javascript) for beginners to partake in coding similar to Logo's Turtle Talk in that it allows easy entry. Scratch allows programming of a digital object (a sprite) similar to the screen version of the Turtle in Logo, and both allow programming of physical objects to provide the "object-to-think-with" paradigm.

The developers of Scratch have been transparent about the influences on the design of the platform. They recount how Logo fell short of living up to its early promise, due in part to the difficulty of the programming language syntax, and noted Papert's position that programming languages need to have a "low floor" (easy for beginners) and a "high ceiling" (capable of facilitating more complex projects over time). They identified their three core design principles in the Scratch design as follows: 1) more *tinkerable*, 2) more *meaningful*, and 3) more *social* than other programming environments (Resnick et al., 2009). The *tinkerable* principle was inspired by the success of Lego blocks in engaging kids and led to the drag-and-drop block design of the Scratch platform. The *meaningful* principle is expressed in the level of personalization allowed in the creation of projects, and the *social* principle is represented in the sharing capabilities that led to Scratch being called "the YouTube of interactive media" (p. 60). This "Lego meets social media" experiment has turned out to be wildly successful in terms of popularity and participation, prompting other similar block-based coding platforms to emerge (see Figure 1.1).

While K–5 educators have been receptive to bringing block-coding into their classrooms, like many teachers welcomed Logo decades ago, questions arise as

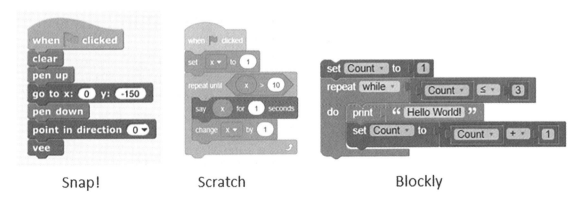

Snap!   Scratch   Blockly

Figure 1.1 Snap!, Scratch, and Blockly drag-and-drop coding.

to the effectiveness of this approach in preparing the computer programmers of the future, and even whether or not that should be the goal. The tension between using programming as a form of expression as opposed to as an onramp to production-oriented languages in K–5 in many ways mirrors the same kind of tension that exists in secondary education. Programming courses using block-based coding in high schools are becoming more prominent and are being taken in lieu of traditional text-based advanced placement courses that have a history of predicting college access. These courses are being lauded for being more engaging and introducing underrepresented students to programming even though the content differs significantly in rigor (Harvard & Howard, 2019; Howard & Harvard, 2019). In both primary and secondary schools, educators have a responsibility to articulate the long-term effects of CS curriculum decisions.

Papert wrote about the responsibility that education has to the tradition of a discipline, asserting that the historical development of the discipline must be considered. He argued that an English teacher would be failing in their duty if they were to invent a new language, write their own poetry, and pass it off to learners in place of traditional works (Papert, 1993). Block coding is not the language of professional programmers, nor are the products of block coding substantively similar to professionally developed computer programs. Block coding is conducted in what Papert referred to as "microworlds," which are simulated knowledge incubators (p. 124) that give learners access to rules, laws, and principles of interest. If such a world creates knowledge that is readily transferable to contexts where the learner will be expected to apply them, then the experiment is a success. If not, then we may have to ask if we are failing in our duty to provide the traditional historical body of CS knowledge.

During the early stages of computers in the classroom, some critics were concerned about the implications of having children compare their thinking to the actions of a computer. There was some fear that students would become robotic in their thinking, as well as less social with their peers. Papert argued that analogizing human thinking to that of a computer is a powerful way to develop procedural thinking abilities for tasks that require them. In his original articulation of computational thinking (CT), he asserted that true computer literacy includes making use of computers and "computational ideas," while also knowing which problems are appropriate for this approach (Papert, 1980; Zhang & Nouri, 2019). Computational thinking was revived in CS research literature by the oft-cited article by Jeanette Wing (2006); however, what followed its publication were multiple definition interpretations of CT over many years, including a clarification from Wing herself (2011) where she defined it as "the thought processes involved in formulating problems and their solutions so that the solutions are represented in a form that can effectively be carried out by an information-processing agent."

In 2012, researchers at the MIT Media Lab—where Scratch was developed—created a framework for assessing CT that includes the following three dimensions:

Computational concepts (i.e., data, Boolean logic/operators, sequences, conditionals, events, loops, and parallelism)

Computational practices (i.e., being incremental and iterative, abstracting and modularizing, reusing and remixing, testing and debugging)

Computational perspectives (i.e., expressing, connecting, and questioning) (Brennan & Resnick, 2012)

In 2019, Zhang and Nouri utilized this framework to conduct a systematic review of fifty-five empirical studies to evaluate the Scratch platform's effectiveness on learning CT for K–9 students (2019). Given Scratch's dominance as a block-based platform, particularly in elementary grades, this study's findings are particularly relevant to understanding the potential effectiveness of Scratch and other similar block-based coding platforms. Although they concluded that Brennan and Resnick's (2012) framework "can be delivered through the use of Scratch" (p. 18), they identified areas of strengths and weaknesses displayed by the participants across research studies. Thoughts and recommendations related to these findings are addressed in the following section; practical examples will offer further guidance in chapters 3, 4, and 5.

Computational Thinking Concepts

Variables

Given that elementary-age students often have little or no programming experience, acquiring a foundation in the basic core programming concepts is essential for building proficiency. Perhaps the most basic concept in programming is variables, since even the simplest of programs will require tracking some information in the computer's memory as the user interacts with the program. This is why programming manuals usually begin with the topic of variables under "Basics" sections (e.g., Whitaker, 2017) and in one instance refers to variables as "one of the most important parts of programming" (p. 25). The fact that variables and functions are listed as prerequisites to advanced-placement programming courses in high school speaks to the importance of understanding variables as a foundation to successful programming.

Citing results from several of the twenty studies in their review that specifically examined the use of data in Scratch programming, Zhang and Nouri (2019) concluded: "Regarding variables, the evidence in the literature points towards students' poor understanding of the concept and reveals the low ability to integrate variables and artefacts." This finding highlights an opportunity for elementary teachers to provide more emphasis on understanding variables in mathematics instruction to support students' acquisition of basic programming concepts. There is evidence that children as young as six years old are capable of thinking in terms of variables (Blanton et al., 2017) and even suggests that introducing the concept earlier may help to avoid difficulty in understanding it later.

Operators

Another core concept in programming, and one that aligns strongly with math instruction, is operators. Mathematics operators in programming are usually straightforward as long as the learner has acquired understanding of add, subtract, multiply, and divide, in which case it is simply a matter of substituting some symbols. For example, the math operators +, -, x, and ÷ are represented in several programming languages as +, -, *, and /, respectively. Relational operators (e.g., <, >, =, >=, <=) are used in code in much the same way they are used in mathematics. Boolean logic operators (e.g., And, Or, Not) are evaluated in terms of being true or false, and they are useful both in decision trees and database searches. Programmers need to understand the difference between statements like "a And b", "a Or b", and "Not (a And b)". Preparing learners for using such operators can be accomplished in mathematics by the use of word problems. For example, a young learner may be capable of understanding that the statement "It's not going to rain and snow" can still be interpreted as it may rain, or it may snow, but both won't happen. Representing this simple example as a "Not (a And b)" situation provides foundation for later understanding a Boolean expression in programming.

Another type of operator that is instrumental in programming is an *assignment operator*, which is used to assign values to variables in code. The foundation of the assignment operator can be found in the use of variables in mathematics when we say let "$x = 5$". Even early in K–5 education, we learn to use this information to calculate "$x + 2$". Assigning values to variables will be among the basic core building blocks of the beginning of coding in any programming language.

Although there are many other operators available in various programming languages, those previously listed represent basic foundational operators that all programmers would be expected to acquire. Zhang and Nouri (2019) found mixed results among the eleven articles that examined the use of Boolean logic operators in Scratch. One study showed good improvement among Scratch users in understanding Boolean logic, whereas another showed only about half of the students examined able to answer questions using the OR operator. Another study showed low use of operators, and another revealed that students could not set Boolean expressions without a teacher's help. Given the extensive use of Boolean expressions in decision-making code syntax, attention must be given to this apparent learning gap.

Algorithms/Sequences

Computer programs are especially well-suited to handle algorithms. If an algorithm, or specific sequence, is coded properly, the end user can expect it to execute exactly the same way every time it runs. Programs that contain data usually manipulate the data using coded algorithms, a task that maps well onto algorithmic computations students execute in mathematics exercises. Scratch users have been found to perform significantly better at these tasks following their work with the platform, showing the ability to recreate the sequences required to perform activities observed from watching a completed program execute (Zhang & Nouri, 2019). Although this activity does not provide experience with syntax that would be observed in a text-based programming language, at a conceptual level it demonstrates students' ability to understand sequencing.

Events

Today's computer applications are expected to engage the user interactively, often requiring the program to react to some action by the user, which programs refer to as *events*. The handling of events in a programming setting involves providing instructions as to what a program is to do if a specific trigger arises. For example, determining what code a program will execute when a user clicks on a particular button or graphic is basic event-handling in programming. Again, this is an activity that is likely better grasped in a programming context than in mathematics instruction. Students were found to be learning how to use simple events as they showed up in the vast majority of studies examined by Zhang and Nouri (2019); however, there was a low usage rate in the studies and not much evidence of the use of complicated events. This is a concept that can be enhanced through flowcharting or in unplugged programming activities.

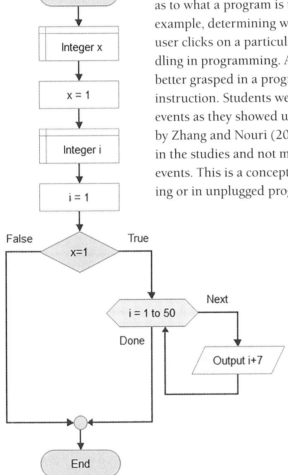

Figure 1.2 Conditionals.

Conditionals

Any program that is more than just a predetermined script will require code to enable it to make decisions based on some interpretable outcome. That outcome could be a certain value having been assigned to a variable, or an event of some kind being triggered. Code utilized to make decisions based on user input or activity usually necessitates the use of *conditional statements* (or just *conditionals*) to accomplish this task (See Figure 1.2). This area has been investigated widely, as examined in twenty-four studies in the Zhang and Nouri (2019) review, and there was evidence of improved ability to use conditionals and control the flow of programs in the Scratch environment. It is possible that a programming context is better suited for teaching conditionals because it is an applied use of the concept to accomplish a programmatic goal. However, conditionals can also be modeled effectively through the use of flowcharts or unplugged programming activities.

Loops

Loops are a mainstay of programming, allowing far more efficiency in programming tasks that must be repeated until a desired result is achieved. For example, if a programmer wants the program to perform a task repeatedly a certain number of times but wants the user to determine that number at runtime, the code would utilize a "for-loop", accepting user input to set the number of intervals. In Scratch terminology, the coder could use an "ask" block to get user input on how many times the sprite should follow a certain sequence. In that case, the code would contain a "repeat" block to encapsulate the loop containing the blocks in the sequence. This not only prevents the need for repetitive code, but also avoids restricting the loop to some predetermined maximum number of iterations. While loops provide additional power and flexibility to the programmer, they also present a source of potential errors if not used properly.

Research has shown the use of endless loops in the Scratch environment as a source of many programming errors, where programs get stuck in never-ending loops (Zhang & Nouri, 2019). Varied understanding of different types of loops, particularly nested loops, have often caused confusion, but this confusion has been less prevalent for Scratch users as compared to text-based languages, since loops are easier to identify in a block-based environment (Mladenovi et al., 2017). Perhaps the best analogy for loops in math is summation notation ($\sum_{i=1}^{10} 2i$, e.g., meaning the summation of all values of $2i$, starting with 1 and ending with 10); this concept is usually not covered until secondary school. Flowcharting, which will be covered in chapter 4 provides a more intuitive, graphical way of representing loops and is therefore recommended over math analogies.

Parallelism/Concurrency

Writing programs beyond simple linear scripts requires sequences of instructions to run concurrently at times, with multiple tasks or activities occurring simultaneously. This *parallelism* not only allows for more efficient use of the vast computing power available in modern computers, but also provides for a much richer and more complex experience for the end user. An interactive user environment will typically need to be able to respond to multiple types of input at a time or to execute multiple actions in code concurrently. For example, a program may require some form of animation to occur simultaneously with accompanying audio; each may be controlled by separate code snippets. As the number of activities increases, the programming may become quite complex to ensure proper coordination.

A total of twelve research articles in Zhang & Nouri's (2019) review examined the ability of students using Scratch to demonstrate parallelism, and the results were mixed. Whereas in some studies students were able to include examples of parallelism in their projects, one study found that the vast majority of students (92.5%) were unable to define concurrency; other studies showed low frequency of the use of concurrency in those projects examined. Intuitively grasping the concept of parallelism in the context of a program is not too difficult; students understand what it means for two things to happen at the same time. However, understanding and using this concept in a programming environment requires recognition of how separate tasks are compartmentalized within that environment.

In the Scratch environment, simply stacking multiple actions inside the same control block, or dragging block sequences to separate stacks, can produce parallelism. In text-based programming environments, such concurrency is accomplished with multithreaded code and requires more abstract thinking to coordinate. Parallelism is a concept that can be developed by students over time as they become more comfortable with programming principles, while flowcharting exercises can help them to visualize concurrent processes. In addition, as students later learn to work with professional visual programming environments such as Microsoft Visual Studio or Eclipse, they can use concurrency visualizer tools to provide support for grasping how parallel code operates in their written programs.

Computational Thinking Practices

Computational thinking practices go beyond the specific content that a learner may be studying and involve metacognitive-level analyses of how one is learning (Brennan & Resnick, 2012). As such, these practices and the thinking behind them extend to other subject matter areas as well. The four sets of practices identified in the Brennan and Resnick framework are briefly described in the following section, along with the kinds of classroom activities that may enhance those practices.

Being Incremental and Iterative

Writing a program to solve a problem or achieve a goal is much like many other substantive school projects in that they are not completed in a straightforward or linear fashion. Whether writing a story, completing a science project, or writing a computer application, an adaptive mindset is needed. It is important that students understand that iterative cycles are a natural part of the programming process, sometimes requiring a change of plans midstream. As with multiple drafts of an essay, a computer program will improve with multiple iterations of revising the structure of the code, utilizing more efficient syntax and eliminating unnecessary elements. This practice will be honed within the normal context of writing programs. This was the least-often assessed practice in Zhang and Nouri's (2019) review, only being assessed specifically in two of the studies reviewed. However, those studies found evidence that students were acquiring the perseverance to code incrementally in the natural process of developing Scratch-based projects.

Abstracting and Modularizing

Although Brennan and Resnick's framework (2012) suggests evaluating abstracting and modularizing together, other frameworks define and evaluate the two practices separately (Zhang & Nouri, 2019). Webb and Rosson (2013) noted that the level of abstraction used in programming can vary in complexity from the simple use of variables to the more complex design of searching-and-sorting procedures. They worked with students presumed to be on the cusp between concrete and abstract thinking and found that they had difficulty in grasping abstraction while using Scratch and Alice platforms. Better abstraction skills can be anticipated as students gain experience with tasks requiring more complex levels of abstraction, which are more commonplace in text-based programming platforms.

Modularizing has been defined as "the breaking down of tasks and procedures into simpler, manageable units that can be combined to create a more complex process" (Bers, 2018, as cited in Zhang & Nouri, 2019). Well-written code is typically modular, meaning code sequences designed for specific tasks will exist in their own separate modules to be called on and executed as needed. This may require multiple modules to be on standby to respond to any event that calls their respective names. Programs typically have *modules* (also referred to as procedures, methods, functions, or subprograms in different programming languages) that may be called upon several times as a program is executing. This structure eliminates the duplication of code that would be used to recreate the module's code in every instance it is needed; it also reduces the chances of errors. It allows for the modules of code to be executed in any order depending on user and program interactions. Analogous to breaking down math problems into smaller units to solve them, young programmers can expect to develop strategies to break their programming projects down into smaller programming tasks as they gain more coding experience.

Remixing and Reusing

Beginning and expert programmers alike can benefit greatly from online communities of shared code produced by others. The use of shared projects in the Scratch platform is analogous to online code repositories used by professional programmers such as Github and Bitbucket. Such repositories eliminate the need for "reinventing the wheel" by allowing you to download publicly shared code modules and tailor them to your specific needs. Within the Scratch environment, reusing and remixing code shared by other users were found to be popular practices. This bodes well for learners using online repositories while transitioning to other platforms. However, this is an area that requires further research (Zhang & Nouri, 2019).

Debugging and Testing

As part of the iterative programming process, students are expected to gain proficiency with testing their creations to see if they perform as expected; this is followed by a cyclic process of revising and retesting until their desired outcomes are attained. Fortunately, the incentive to learn debugging is built into the process. Once students invest in a project by way of planning, coding properties and events, curating shared modularized work, and adding their personal touches to a program, they usually can't wait to test it in order to get immediate feedback. This is an area where students can feel they are getting objective feedback irrespective of any biases or stereotypes that may exist in a classroom setting. If they code their project correctly, the fact that it runs correctly makes it a success. If it does not, they can rest assured that this is an objective assessment, and they can feel encouraged that success will come if they figure out and correct their mistakes.

Testing and debugging was the most frequently observed practice in Scratch programming research. Though students demonstrated success in learning to iteratively correct and improve their work products, understanding of debugging was found to develop slowly in the early stages. Such findings suggest that the introduction of programming at younger ages is a positive development in that it gives them more time to develop debugging and other practices that require time to master.

This further aligns with expectations related to perseverance addressed in the Common Core State Mathematics Standards.

Computational Thinking Perspectives

Brennan and Resnick (2012) included a perspectives dimension in their CT framework to capture some of the personal shifts they observed in students' understanding of selves and in relationships to the people and technology in their lives. This dimension is particularly important when evaluating the effects of engagement with computational experiences by young learners who are likely to shape their motivational and affective responses to the early exposure. There are three elements to the perspectives dimension: expressing, connecting, and questioning. Expressing captures the transition students make to thinking of technology as a medium through which they can express themselves. The control they are able to exert over their projects through programming allows their work to be extensions of themselves, making them highly personal. The connecting element is a byproduct of the sharing culture built within the Scratch website, encouraging and supporting networks of students in developing their knowledge base and proficiency. Finally, the questioning element arises from a sense of empowerment developed as students learn how complex systems work. Approaching their work as creators, rather than receptors or consumers, cultivates a mindset of wanting to design rather than be subject to their surrounding environment. Such an experience can be viewed as a culturally responsive approach to learning. We will cover more of this learning methodology in chapter 2.

The perspectives dimension does not involve specific concepts or practices, which explains why Zhang and Nouri (2019) found just six or fewer studies investigating each of the dimension's elements. Nonetheless, they offer a lens with which to frame educators' thinking when trying to shape the culture of their infusion of CS in elementary classrooms. Our goals should be more than just mastering CT concepts and practices; they should include cultivating the perspectives that will determine whether students ever seriously entertain the pursuit of STEM careers in general or computer programming in particular. Furthermore, a positive experience in problem-solving activities can go a long way in encouraging students to transfer their learned CT approaches to problem-solving in other domains.

A Look Ahead

The research discussed in this chapter has illuminated various levels of success that students have experienced in acquiring CT concepts, practices, and perspectives while engaging in block-based programming approaches in classroom settings. It should be noted that, despite its prevalence in elementary CS curricula, there are differing views on whether drag-and-drop, block-based programming is the best way to bring CS into K–12 education. The differing views are based, in large part, on how one defines their purpose for the inclusion of programming-based CS into the curriculum. At the elementary school level, emphasis has been placed on providing a curriculum that is accessible and engaging enough to stimulate interest in CS for a wider range of students than previously observed. The core design principles of Scratch—"more tinkerable, more meaningful, and more social than other programming environments" (Resnick et al., 2009, p. 63)—suggest a purpose centered on self-expression and personal relevance in order to keep students engaged. The designers vow to keep Scratch's primary focus on lowering the floor for successful entry to coding, expanding access to a more diverse group of students, but not raising the ceiling of what can be achieved through programming. The designers assert that for students "who see programming as a medium for expression, not a path toward a career, Scratch is sufficient for their needs" (p. 67).

This brings us to a different potential purpose for bringing CS into education: to leverage curiosity and provide opportunities whereby students can identify personal interests and establish a foundation for a possible career in programming-related CS fields. This longer view of purpose must consider the impact that block-based curricula can have on students' future coursework and aspirations in CS—in secondary school and beyond. In this view it is important to know whether the lower "floor" that block-based coding provides adequately prepares them for a transition into secondary school or into real-world programming environments. The designers of Scratch acknowledge that, "For some Scratchers, especially those who want to pursue a career in programming or computer science, it is important to move on to other languages" (Resnick et al., 2009, p. 66).

For educators who see the purpose of education in general, and CS in particular, as a road toward preparing students for successful CS-related careers in life, learning core CS concepts and practices in a manner that this knowledge can be built upon for professional success may take precedence over activities centered on self-expression and tinkering. These educators must have clarity as to their mission when deciding on which approach best serves the mission. This is not to say that we must choose one and discard the other, but it does suggest that the platform one chooses to build their students' CS foundation upon is not a neutral decision, but rather can have important implications for years to come.

The chapters that follow will delve deeper into the concepts and practices outlined in the CT framework, providing some alternative approaches to bringing coding into the K–5 classroom. These approaches utilize a variety of means, including text-based programming and unplugged activities; they also seek to strengthen math skills in the process. Although we will discuss programming activities, our focus will not be limited to any specific programming language or platform. We will, how-ever, address the kinds of core concepts and practices common to most program-ming languages. Students develop at different rates and have varying interest levels in CS. Many will be ready and interested at some point on the K–5 continuum in moving past the tinkering and self-expression in block-based platforms and will thrive in serious syntax-based programming if given the opportunity. Chapter 2 will outline the relevant standards you might consider integrating into lessons, while chapters 3, 4, and 5 will provide examples of both block-based and text-based pro-gramming approaches to teaching core CT concepts and practices. We leave it up to the individual educator to determine where the transition will occur, but encourage gaining input on the matter from the students and their parents as to what kind of CS they want to experience. When CS programs are being touted to students and parents as early pathways into lucrative STEM careers, it should be clear which opportunities are centered on self-expression, on platforms not used in the real world of computing, and which are providing truly transferable foundational skills used to design the programs and products we use every day.

Former technology coach and current principal at Pomona Unified School District, Veronica Godinez, highlights the importance of involving parents in the rollout of innovative technology in an elementary school. She recognized that parents might not be familiar with the kinds of activities their children were sharing with them, so she got out ahead of any possible concerns by inviting the parents to the school to share in those experiences. Her students were using drag-and-drop coding to program robots, giving rise to the thought that they were doing more playing than learning. Similar concerns can arise when students use drag-and-drop coding to program animated sprites, especially when there isn't much *code* evident in their work products. We encourage educators to share the rationale for curriculum deci-sions, as Ms. Godinez so adeptly did, and involve parents when choosing between curricula with coding as a form of expression vs. coding for CS field preparation.

Involving Parents in Coding Success

VERONICA GODINEZ

In March of 2016, I had the privilege of attending the CUE Spring Conference in Palm Springs. The keynote speaker for that year was Hadi Partovi, the founder of Code. org. A light was ignited in me as he shared with the audience his personal story, the data on computer science in schools, and the need for positions to be filled. That year I was serving as an instructional technology coach at an elementary school. I had a supportive leadership team and staff, and it was the beginning of my new year with Tech Tykes (TK-3 students) and my Tech Gurus (4–6 students). To get started, I created coding clubs after school, and each group had two days in the computer lab with me. We created, we collaborated, we persevered, and most importantly, we had so much fun learning together.

Funding was low, but that didn't stop me. We used all the free coding programs available. After a year of coding on Code.org and Scratch, I felt there was something missing: application! I needed them to apply the code that they had learned. An idea was born, so I wrote a proposal to DonorsChoose, and my project was funded. I had the opportunity to purchase two Dash & Dot robot sets. I then went a step further. During student lunches, I opened up my classroom to the students. I gave each teacher two to three passes for their students, and twice a week during their lunch they had the opportunity to learn with my robots, code on the computers, or collaborate on littleBits STEAM sets.

Students would quickly eat their lunch and line up outside my door—exited to get started. One of their favorite games to play was Math Capture the Kingdom with Dash. I had searched for math lessons and finally found the perfect one that I could use while involving the majority of the class. *All* students would have the opportunity to solve a math problem, collaborate, and have fun. It is similar to the popular game Capture the Flag. I'd divide the class into two teams with approximately twelve students in each group. Each team was given a Dash and an iPad to program the robot. The object of the game was to program the robots to land on coordinates on the map and to solve math problems placed at each coordinate. Students earned points for solving each math problem. Aside from collecting points, students needed to work together to get to the other side of the map. I added one rule to the game: if the robots crashed into each other, the team that had written the code and used it to program the robot would need to give their points to the other team. While students played the game, I was the facilitator. I gave them two key guidelines: 1) *everyone* needs to participate, and 2) students need to work together to solve problems. It was a magical learning opportunity to see those as young as first grade verbalizing their thoughts, persevering, and collaborating to accomplish their goal.

Children would go home and share with parents that the teacher on campus was bringing her robots to class to play. In order to diffuse any negative concerns around coding and CS, I invited the parents to an informational session on the importance of teaching *all* students CS. I shared with parents all the updated data that Hadi Partovi had shared, but I also gave the parents the opportunity to participate in the Hour of Code. I set the timer and did activities similar to what I would do with the students. I facilitated and allowed them to work together and learn. Throughout the session, I noticed a few similar things that took place during both the student and parent sessions. I heard laughter, I saw parents helping other parents, and so much more. When the timer went off one hour later, parents did the same thing the students had done: complained about how they wanted more time.

Around this time of year, I was selected to be a part of the Computer Science Standards Advisory Committee that would oversee the writing of the standards. Along with 20 other passionate educators from across the state of California, the Golden California Computer Science Standards were created. The purpose of the Advisory Committee was to create a set of standards that would cohesively align with NGSS and Common Core ELA and Math Standards. The CS Advisory Committee spent many hours aligning the standards to other Core subjects and even added suggestions for lesson ideas. Along with the standards, the progression chart was created spanning from kindergarten to twelfth grade and through to specialty courses. We wanted teachers to have a comprehensive resource.

Since 2016, I continue to create and initiate coding clubs for ALL students. They are never too young or too old to learn about CS. Computer science teaches students how to problem-solve and collaborate with others, and it also builds empathy and encourages students to be creative critical thinkers.

 Mission Clarity

Programming languages and platforms will continue to come and go. Those that remain will undergo revisions and updates as time goes on. We do not want to limit the reach of this core knowledge to a specific language, but will rather concentrate on the elements of programming expected to endure the test of time. Although code examples are provided to illustrate how certain concepts manifest in practice, the user is encouraged to seek a grasp of the ideas rather than attempting to memorize specific coding syntax. In addition, the Mission Clarity sections in the following chapters will address how their content is related to the two different purposes previously outlined: self-expression and CS education/field preparation. We do not advocate the exclusive adoption of one particular purpose, but encourage school districts, administrators, and teachers to make more than one perspective approach available to students so as not to limit them to a preparation model that does not honor their capabilities or aspirations.

RESOURCES

RESOURCE	SOURCE	ACCESS	
Scratch Home Site	Massachusetts Institute of Technology		(www.mit.edu)
Blockly Reference Site	Google		(developers.google.com/ blockly)
Snap! Reference Site	University of California, Berkeley		(snap.berkeley.edu/index)

RESOURCE	SOURCE	ACCESS	
Unplugged Activities for Hour of Code	TeachHUB.com		(teachhub.com/4-unplugged-classroom-activities-hour-code)
Visual Studio Development Platform Site	Microsoft Corporation		(visualstudio.microsoft.com)
Eclipse Development Platform Site	Eclipse Foundation		(eclipse.org)
Donors Choose Organization Site	DonorsChoose.org, a 501(c)(3)		(donorschoose.org)
littleBits Site	Sphero Inc.		(littlebits.com/pages/about)
K12 Computer Science	Defining Computer Science		(k12cs.org/defining-computer-science)

CHAPTER

2

Focusing the Learning

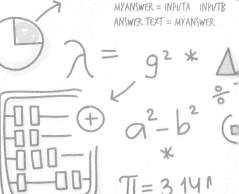

This chapter addresses the background and importance of the Common Core State Standards for Mathematics (CCSSM), CS standards from the Computer Science Teachers Association (CSTA), as well as ISTE Computational Thinking Competencies and their Computer Science Standards for Educators. In addition to addressing the background information of various standards, this chapter highlights several specific standards that will be referenced in subsequent chapters. When appropriate, similarities between CCSSM standards and different international mathematics standards are also discussed to help inform instructional decisions for educators across the globe. Finally, this chapter covers how to establish a positive classroom environment and key pedagogical tips for math and CS instruction.

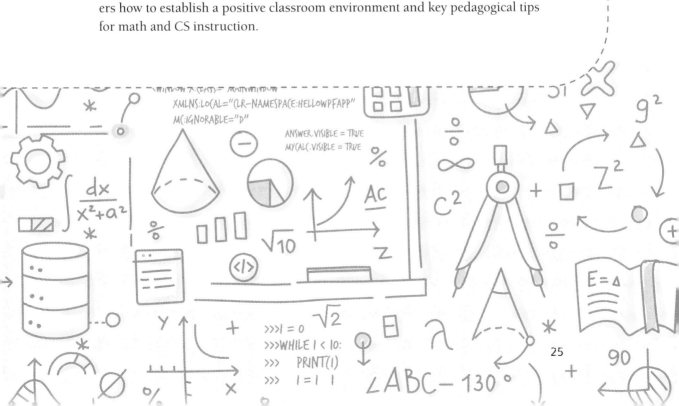

25

What About the Standards?

Standards are often used to drive instruction or to ensure students are on pace to progress to their next grade level. Utilizing standards when lesson-planning can create a learning focus for students. However, standards should not be used in a way that presents a hurdle for academic growth or stifles a student's creativity. Educators should leverage local math and CS standards to open doors of curiosity and opportunity. Coupling local math and CS standards with ISTE Computational Thinking Competencies and/or Computer Science Standards for Educators enhances the teaching and learning experience and eliminates the barriers that commonly prohibit students from deeply exploring new math and CS concepts. In addition to leveraging the use of standards to focus learning, establishing a positive classroom environment and implementing sound pedagogical practices are essential elements for the successful facilitation of instruction.

Understanding the CCSSM

The development of the CCSSM was based on the identified need to better prepare students for college and careers by forty-eight state leaders who came together after recognizing a lack of agreement about "the level at which a student is determined to be sufficiently educated at each grade level" and "the value of consistent, real-world learning goals" (National Governors Association Center for Best Practices, corestandards.org, 2010). The CCSSM were informed by existing math standards from individual states, the expertise of teachers, content-area experts, thought leaders, and nearly 10,000 comments from the public (e.g., parents, concerned citizens). Once the standards were developed, states went through their various processes to determine whether to adopt the CCSSM. To date, approximately thirty-five U.S. states maintain Common Core adoption.

CCSSM are used by educators and curriculum designers to help focus math lessons to ensure students are on track for promotion to their next grade level and graduation and are prepared for college, future careers, and life. Although some educators grapple with using a standardized tool for learning, the CCSSM can potentially promote equity when applied as a guide instead of driving lessons at a pace that hinders students from grasping the foundational concepts behind math procedures. Throughout subsequent chapters, specific CCSSM standards will be presented in project examples. The following Common Core Standards for Mathematical Practice will also be addressed to support the

Access the CCSM.
(corestandards.org/
Math/Practice)

conceptual understanding of the connections between the CCSSM and CS in K–5 math instruction:

- Make sense of problems and persevere in solving them (CCSS.Math.Practice.MP1)

- Reason abstractly and quantitatively (CCSS.Math.Practice.MP2)

- Construct viable arguments and critique the reasoning of others (CCSS.Math.Practice.MP3)

- Model with mathematics (CCSS.Math.Practice.MP4)

- Use appropriate tools strategically (CCSS.Math.Practice.MP5)

- Attend to precision (CCSS.Math.Practice.MP6)

- Look for and make use of structure (CCSS.Math.Practice.MP7)

- Look for and express regularity in repeated reasoning (CCSS.Math.Practice.MP8)

Computer Science Standards for Students

The K–12 Computer Science Framework (2016) has been utilized to inform the instructional design of CS curricula in various states and districts. It has also been used in the development of the Computer Science Teachers Association (CSTA) K–12 Computer Science Standards. The concept statements and practices outlined

Table 2.1   **K–12 CS Framework Concepts and Practices**

CONCEPTS	PRACTICES
1. Computing Systems	1. Fostering an Inclusive Computing Culture
2. Networks and the Internet	2. Collaborating Around Computing
3. Data and Analysis	3. Recognizing and Defining Computational Problems
4. Algorithms and Programming	4. Developing and Using Abstractions
5. Impacts of Computing	5. Creating Computational Artifacts
	6. Testing and Refining Computational Artifacts
	7. Communicating About Computing

next from the K–12 Computer Science Framework were utilized to craft the CSTA K–12 Computer Science Standards (table 2.1).

Access the K–12 Computer Science Framework.

(k12cs.org)

In July 2017, CSTA released their revised K–12 Computer Science Standards with the goal of delineating "a core set of learning objectives designed to provide the foundation for a complete computer science curriculum" (CSTA, 2017). In addition, CSTA continues to strengthen their network of K–12 CS teachers through the creation of local communities across the U.S. and Canada. Given the fact that not all states in the U.S., or territories in other countries, have adopted a set of CS standards, the CSTA K–12 CS Standards offer a coherent and comprehensive set of standards that educators can use as a guide in their teaching and learning.

According to the csteachers.org website, the CSTA K–12 Standards introduce the fundamental concepts of CS to students, present CS at a graduation-credit-worthy level for secondary students, and encourage the offering of secondary-level CS courses that prepare all students for college and/or the workforce. Throughout the subsequent chapters, the CSTA Standards for grades K–5 will be presented in project examples. Abbreviated examples of descriptive statements for various standards under each of the domains, as outlined in the K–5 section of the CSTA K–12 CS Standards, are presented in Table 2.2. The goal is to further support the conceptual understanding of the connections between the CCSSM Standards, Mathematical Practice Concepts, and CS in K–5 mathematics instruction.

ISTE Computational Thinking Competencies

According to ISTE (2019), the CT Competencies "focus on the educator knowledge, skills and mindsets to integrate computational thinking across K–12 content areas with students of every age." As previously noted in chapter 1, CT is an important element of CS, and when utilized appropriately it can effectively support student interest and learning. ISTE has been clear that the CT Competencies are not a "one-size-fits-all list of expectations"; rather, the purpose is to give educators a framework whereby they can set goals for teaching and learning. "The ISTE Computational Thinking Competencies are designed to prepare students with the skills needed to solve problems of the future," said ISTE CEO Richard Culatta (via iste.org, 2018). Following are the ISTE Standards for Educators: Computational Thinking Competencies:

- Computational Thinking (Learner)

- Equity Leader (Leader)

- Collaborating Around Computing (Collaborator)

- Creativity and Design (Designer)

- Integrating Computational Thinking (Facilitator)

Access the ISTE CT Competencies.
(iste.org/standards/ computational- thinking)

The ISTE Standards for Students are also an important guide for educators, as they support students with strengthening math skills through CS. The Computational Thinker strand calls for "students [to] develop and employ strategies for understanding and solving problems in ways that leverage the power of technological methods to develop and test solutions" (iste.org, 2019). This particular strand is outlined in the following section to offer a quick visual reference for what can be used in the classroom to help guide instruction:

- Students formulate problem definitions suited for technology-assisted methods such as data analysis, abstract models, and algorithmic thinking in exploring and finding solutions. (5a)

- Students collect data or identify relevant data sets, use digital tools to analyze them, and represent data in various ways to facilitate problem-solving and decision-making. (5b)

- Students break problems into component parts, extract key information, and develop descriptive models to understand complex systems or facilitate problem-solving. (5c)

- Students understand how automation works and use algorithmic thinking to develop a sequence of steps to create and test automated solutions. (5d)

CSTA/ISTE Computer Science Standards for Educators

In 2019, CSTA and ISTE released a revised set of Standards for Computer Science Educators to outline what educators should know and do in order to efficiently support students in their acquisition of new knowledge. As outlined in the K–12 Computer Science Framework and CSTA's K–12 Computer Science Standards, educators are expected to demonstrate a clear and flexible understanding of the same concepts outlined for students: 1) Computing Systems, 2) Networks and the Internet, 3) Data and Analysis, 4) Algorithms and Programming, and 5) Impacts of Computing. In order to demonstrate knowledge in the above areas, K–5 educators may benefit from understanding the CSTA/ISTE Standards for Educators even if CS is not their sole content area. The following CSTA/ISTE Computer Science

Table 2.2 **CSTA Abbreviated Descriptive Statements for CS Standards**

DOMAINS	LEVEL 1A: GRADES K-2 (AGES 5-7)	LEVEL 1B: GRADES 3-5 (AGES 8-11)
Computing Systems	Students should be able to identify and describe the function of external hardware, such as desktop computers, laptop computers, tablet devices, monitors, keyboards, mice, and printers. (Hardware & Software: 1A-CS-02)	At this stage, a model should only include the basic elements of a computer system, such as input, output, processor, sensors, and storage. Students could draw a model on paper or in a drawing program, program an animation to demonstrate it, or demonstrate it by acting this out in some way. (Hardware & Software: 1B-CS-02)
Networks and the Internet	Learning to protect one's device or information from unwanted use by others is an essential first step in learning about cybersecurity. Students are not required to use multiple strong passwords. They should appropriately use and protect the passwords they are required to use. (Cybersecurity: 1A-NI-04)	Students should demonstrate their understanding of the flow of information by, for instance, drawing a model of the way packets are transmitted, programming an animation to show how packets are transmitted, or demonstrating this through an unplugged activity that has them act it out in some way. (Network Communication & Organization: 1B-NI-04)
Data and Analysis	All information stored and processed by a computing device is referred to as data. Data can be images, text documents, audio files, software programs or apps, video files, etc. As students use software to complete tasks on a computing device, they will be manipulating data. (Storage: 1A-DA-05)	A data set of sports teams could be sorted by wins, points scored, or points allowed, and a data set of weather information could be sorted by high temperatures, low temperatures, or precipitation. (Collection Visualization & Transformation: 1B-DA-06)

DOMAINS	LEVEL 1A: GRADES K-2 (AGES 5-7)	LEVEL 1B: GRADES 3-5 (AGES 8-11)
Algorithms and Programming	Loops allow for the repetition of a sequence of code multiple times. For example, in a program to show the life cycle of a butterfly, a loop could be combined with move commands to allow continual but controlled movement of the character. (Control: 1A-AP-10)	Variables are used to store and modify data. At this level, understanding how to use variables is sufficient. For example, students may use mathematical operations to add to the score of a game or subtract from the number of lives available in a game. The use of a variable as a countdown timer is another example. (Variables: 1B-AP-09)
Impacts of Computing	Students could share their work on blogs or in other collaborative spaces online, taking care to avoid sharing information that is inappropriate or that could personally identify them to others. Students could provide feedback to others on their work in a kind and respectful manner and could tell an adult if others are sharing things they should not share or are treating others in an unkind or disrespectful manner on online collaborative spaces. (Social Interactions: 1A-IC-17)	Computing provides the possibility for collaboration and sharing of ideas and allows the benefit of diverse perspectives. For example, students could seek feedback from other groups in their class or students at another grade level. Or, with guidance from their teacher, they could use video conferencing tools or other online collaborative spaces, such as blogs, wikis, forums, or website comments, to gather feedback from individuals and groups about programming projects. (Social Interactions: 1B-IC-20)

Standards for Educators are broadly addressed through the subsequent chapters in this book.

- Knowledge of Computer Science for Teaching
- Equity Advocate
- Professional Growth and Identity
- Educator as CS Instructional Designer
- CS Classroom Practitioner

Access the standards for CS teachers.

(csteachers.org/ page/standards-for-cs-teachers)

What these standards can offer K–5 educators is a gentle reminder on how to be effective in their teaching practice when integrating CS. For example, under the Knowledge of Computer Science for Teaching domain, a set of professional and CT practices are included as a guide for expanding knowledge in emerging areas of CS (Table 2.3).

Table 2.3 **Knowledge of CS for Teaching Domain**

Demonstrate CS Practices

PROFESSIONAL CS PRACTICES	COMPUTATIONAL THINKING PRACTICES
1. Fostering an inclusive computing culture	1. Recognizing and defining computational problems
2. Collaborating around computing	2. Developing and using abstractions
3. Communicating about computing	3. Creating computational artifacts
	4. Testing and refining computational artifacts

This particular set of standards calls for CS educators to build community and remain open to learning new areas of CS while understanding the ethical, social, economic, and cultural contexts in which they operate. Elementary educators who are integrating CS also serve to benefit from applying these practices. The story of Ari Flewelling, a former staff development specialist in Riverside Unified School District, demonstrates the journey of an educator who exhibits flexible knowledge in CS and continued interest in learning emerging CS areas.

Growing Into and Through CS

ARI FLEWELLING

Growing up, I was always interested in technology, and I was fortunate that my dad would bring home old computers from work. He inspired my curiosity, love, and "click all the buttons" attitude toward technology. When I was in college, I needed a part-time job, and the information technology help desk was hiring student workers—a perfect fit for me. As an extrovert, it was great getting to interact with people from across the university. Unfortunately, even though I was interested in computer science and earned high marks in college-level intro-to-computing classes, I majored in English. I wished I could have remembered some of what my dad had taught me growing up. Luckily for me, it all worked out for the best.

I originally started my career as a high school English teacher and was always finding ways to integrate technology into my curriculum. In light of my experiences at the help desk and teaching, I was able to transition to teaching other teachers about integrating technology. In my role as a staff development specialist, I help grades PK–12 teachers learn about various ways to incorporate technology into the classroom, including physical computing, virtual/augmented reality, cloud computing, and design think-ing. My favorite days are when I'm in the field coaching teachers and working with students. I love leading teacher professional development, because getting to talk with teachers about their educational practice and how they can enhance the lives of students is exhilarating and makes me hopeful for the future.

However, even in this capacity, up until 2018 I didn't think of myself as a CS educator. I earned my teaching credential in English, not math, science, or CS, and because of this I wasn't always welcome in the CS space. So I thought I was a supporter, not an active participant in CS. However, at the encouragement of my manager, I applied for the NCWIT Aspirations in Computing (AiC) Educator Inland Empire Award. He saw something in my work that I did not. Applying for the award was an intimidating pro-cess because I didn't think I was worthy of the award. However, as I began reviewing the application, I realized I was doing more than I thought. Through partnerships with the county office, I helped host events advocating for CS, and within my district, I lead our partnership with Girls Who Code. I thought because I wasn't coding with kids every day, I wasn't doing computer science work. Nevertheless, the Inland Empire Chapter of NCWIT selected me as the winner due to my advocacy for CS with teachers, students, and the education community at large.

This award is so important to me because it reminds me that despite not being an expert in this field, I can still help others and make a positive impact on the CS community at large. I like to share this story because I feel it helps others realize that anyone can get involved with CS. In addition, it reminds me how important it is to have an advocate in your corner telling you what you can do with enough support and effort. When I was young, it was my dad, and now I'm lucky to be surrounded by other educators who motivate me. I'm in a role where I can help others to ensure another person never feels limited like I did in college and in my early career. I hope as educators we can not only encourage our youngest scholars to explore CS, but that we continue to support them well into their school careers so they can code a better world.

Planning Coding and Math Instruction

As a K–5 educator, learning more about CS content and pedagogical practices is essential. Just as important is obtaining a conceptual understanding about how to plan and implement effective math and CS instruction. What we currently know about pedagogy and coding in elementary classrooms stems from the work of Seymour Papert (1967, 1971, 1980). According to Papert, children should function as creators and playful explorers as they take control of their own learning. As noted in the introduction, Papert's approach to teaching was very much influenced by the constructivist theory of learning, in which Jean Piaget argued that people build knowledge best when actively engaged in learning. Integrating coding and math in lessons provides an ideal opportunity for students to build knowledge conceptually and practically. Papert's ideals challenge educators to avoid compliance or standardization and to push toward encouraging student agency and intellectual freedom (Stager, 2016).

Planning instruction that integrates math and computer science, while fostering agency and intellectual freedom, requires patience and instructional strategies that consistently engage students, such as culturally responsive pedagogy. Researchers have suggested that proper teaching strategies are necessary to support students' learning performance (Chang et al., 2012). Since the integration of math and coding in a single lesson is a developing practice in K–5 classrooms, patience and a positive classroom environment are essential ingredients when planning effective instruction. Below are several tips to focus the learning when planning coding and math instruction.

- **Consider the standards:** Although standards should not drive the pace of your lesson, they can help focus the learning for students.

- **Introduce vocabulary early:** Present new concepts using key vocabulary. Offer students a chance to try using context clues to define new terms before giving them the actual definitions.

- **Plan beyond the lesson:** Embrace the notion that students may progress faster through your lessons than expected. Plan accordingly by developing extension activities.

- **Mix it up:** Plan to deliver content using multiple approaches such as paired programming, project-based learning, peer assessments, modeling, stations, and even a smidge of direct instruction.

- **Offer choice:** Give students the opportunity to select their project platform to demonstrate understanding.

- **Make it real:** Relate the content to students and remember to draw connections to real-world issues.

 # Mission Clarity

Establishing a positive classroom environment must include efforts to relate the content to students and drawing connections to real-world issues. In order to relate the content to students, it is also helpful to utilize culturally responsive pedagogies that leverage the brain's memory systems and information-processing structures (Hammond, 2014). Hammond argued that students from diverse backgrounds may be most familiar with cultural traditions in which their primary ways of transferring knowledge and meaning-making occur in ways observed and enacted by their family. For example, a student most familiar with storytelling is more likely to transfer knowledge and make meaning through oral presentations of their work. This also connects with Brennan and Resnick's *computational thinking perspectives*

(as outlined in chapter 1) and ISTE CT Competencies related to Integrating Computational Thinking (5b) whereby you "empower students to select personally meaningful computational projects" (ISTE, 2019).

Furthermore, allowing students to choose between activities will give them the opportunity to draw from cultural traditions they are most familiar with while demonstrating their strengths and showcasing what they value most. A decision to offer students choices can be viewed as selecting a curriculum path whereby students are allowed room for self-expression while acquiring knowledge that contributes to what may be helpful for the CS field. For example, a grade 3 student who often uses block-based programs may decide to complete a project using a text-based language. In this scenario, the self-expression component is visible in how the teacher offers choice for students to determine how they will demonstrate their understanding of a concept. Although the teacher may have started out down one curriculum pathway, the student may have decided to utilize an advanced programming language. This is an indication that making one curriculum decision whereby students self-express can also include opportunities for them to prepare for the CS field.

RESOURCES

RESOURCE	SOURCE	LINK	
ISTE Computational Thinking Competencies	International Society for Technology in Education		(iste.org/standards/computational-thinking)
Common Core State Standards for Mathematics	Common Core State Standards Initiative		(corestandards.org/Math)
K–12 Computer Science Framework 2016	K–12 Computer Science Framework Steering Committee		(k12cs.org)

RESOURCE	SOURCE	LINK	
CSTA K–12 Computer Science Standards Site	Computer Science Teachers Association		(csteachers.org/page/ standards)
NCWIT Aspirations in Computing	NCWIT Aspirations in Computing		(aspirations.org)

Data
Dialogue

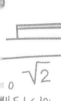

This chapter explores the fundamental concept of data and variables as they relate to coding. Definitions and examples are shared along with a project to explore variables.

Also included in this chapter:

- Definitions of data types and how they are declared in different programming languages
- Standards-aligned variable project using Visual Studio
- Feature: "Coding + Math during Preservice Teacher Development" by Dr. Cory Gleasman
- Resources for learning more about data and variables

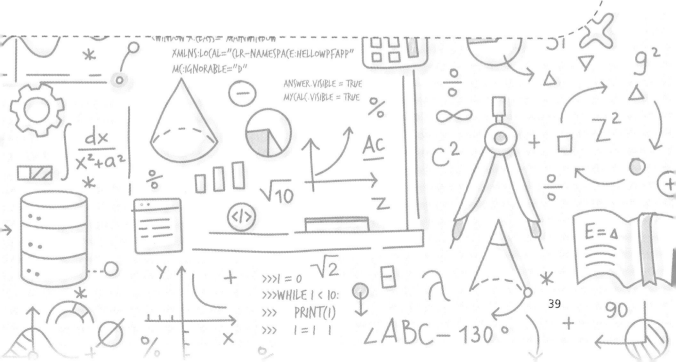

G iven the importance of data as one of the foundational building blocks of any program, it is important that beginning programmers have a solid foundation in how the variables that hold data are created and manipulated in code. Even the best of programming efforts can be derailed by errors related to using variables that are of the incorrect, or incompatible, types for the data being stored in them. However, before we discuss the variables and their types, a quick primer on how computers actually store data, any kind of data, will be helpful in shaping overall understanding of how computer programs work.

All data on computers are represented as a series of binary numbers stored in bits. Binary numbers have only one of two values: 0 or 1. A *bit* is the smallest unit of information storage on a computer; however, the smallest unit that can be given an address by a computer is a *byte*, which is comprised of eight bits. Although having students learn the base-2 system of mathematics is not particularly useful for learning programming, they should at least understand that each data type has a limited number of bytes allocated to it, as well as restrictions on the kinds of data each can store. It needs to be understood that once a section of memory is allocated to a variable, that space cannot be used for any other purpose within that program for the duration it is running. Given that computer memory is a limited resource, it is not possible to allocate unlimited memory to variables, and if too much space is allocated, the increased use of memory runs the risk of slowing the program's execution. Thus, programming languages limit the amount of resources, or bytes, allocated to different types of variables and rely on the programmer to select those appropriate to their program's needs. Beyond memory needs, there is another, more important, reason for selecting the appropriate type of variable. When your program attempts to perform some kind of operation on the data, mistyped data (i.e., data of one type being assigned to a variable of a different type) can lead to program crashes, lost data, or other unexpected results.

There are many variable types across the different programming languages, but most programming tasks that beginning programmers can reasonably expect to encounter can be handled with a small subset of data types that handle the most common forms of data. In a K–5 setting, data in the form of integers, floating decimals, Boolean values, and strings should handle the vast majority of their data storage needs. The integer data type is capable of storing numeric values from about negative two billion to positive two billion, which is more than sufficient to handle a wide range of programming possibilities. The float data type provides even greater numeric data capacity and includes accuracy to seven digits beyond the

Table 3.1   **Declaring Basic Data Types by Programming Language**

TYPE	INTEGER	FLOATING DECIMAL	BOOLEAN	STRING
C	int myCount = 5;	float myPi = 3.14;	int myB1 = 0;	char name[10] = "Bob";
C#	int myCount = 5;	float myPi = 3.14f;	bool myB1 = false;	string name = "Bob";
Python	myCount = 5	myPi = 3.14	myB1 = False	name = "Bob"
Visual Basic	Dim myCount as Integer = 5	Dim myPi as float = 3.14	Dim myB1 as Boolean = 0	Dim name as String = "Bob"
Java	int myCount = 5;	float myPi = 3.14f	Boolean myB1; myB1 = false;	String name = "Bob";
Scratch				

decimal point for fractional values. Programs using fractional numbers written by elementary students would not likely require more precision than a float variable can provide. The frequent use of Boolean logic in programming, testing whether some condition is true or false, makes the Boolean variable type important to understand as an early foundational CT concept as well. Finally, all programs will use the string variable type in some capacity, which stores alphanumeric characters used to communicate with the end user. String variables are stored as text and have a capacity of about one billion characters.

Before using a variable in code, the programmer must *declare* the variable to tell the computer to reserve space for the data that it will hold. In programming languages that are *strongly typed*, the programmer must also specify the type of data that will be stored in the variables at the time they declare them. Table 3.1 provides examples of how the previously described subset of variable types are declared across various languages. Note that Python and Scratch are dynamically typed languages; they set variable types by attempting to interpret the data assigned to them. While this makes using variables quick and easy, it can lead to errors when the programmer crosses types in the handling of data. It also does not require the programmer to consider variable types, which is a skill useful and necessary to work with some other languages. Scratch is the easiest to declare of the examples provided, but it does not require any syntax and its programs only run on the Scratch website. Text-based programming languages require syntax in order to allow the code to run in other platforms and contexts.

In the examples provided in Table 3.1, the terms beginning with "my" are variables that are created and named by the programmer; hence they could be named anything as long as they follow the guidelines for the particular language. In text-based languages, they generally can contain letters, digits, and the underscore character (_). They are case-sensitive (i.e., "score" is different from "Score") and often are required to begin with a letter or an underscore. In addition, text-based programming languages each have a set of keywords that are reserved for a particular purpose (such as *int, float,* and *bool*), and as such, they cannot be used for variable names. Fortunately, many application program interface (API) designs include features that alert the programmer when variable naming conventions aren't followed.

Getting Out the Blocks
Project: Introduction to Variables

 k12stemequity.com/intro-to-variables

Overview

Although instruction on how variables are declared, named, and typed can occur offline in unplugged activities, we encourage allowing students to experiment with creating variables in a computer API so they gain familiarity in an authentic development context. For our project example, we'll use the C# (pronounced "C Sharp") programming language to allow its strongly typed behavior to highlight the differences in how data are handled in code. We will use the Microsoft Visual Studio (MVS) Community Edition (available for free download for PC or Mac at visualstudio.microsoft.com/downloads) to take advantage of its built-in debugging and coding assistance. For this sample lesson, you will need to launch a new project from the MVS file menu and create a Console App using the C# language (see instructions that follow).

Duration

Depending on your students' familiarity with basic coding concepts and Microsoft Visual Studio, they will need approximately forty-five minutes to an hour to complete this project. Allow students to work in pairs when necessary. Consider separating this project into two lessons and give students time on the second day to discuss any obstacles or difficulties encountered while working through their projects.

CODING + MATH

CSTA Standards for CS Educators

- **5c.** Promote student self-efficacy. Facilitate students' engagement in the learning process and encourage students to take leadership of their own learning by encouraging creativity and use of a variety of resources and problem-solving techniques.

- **5e.** Encourage student communication about computing. Create meaningful opportunities for students to discuss, read, and write about computing.

ISTE Standards for Students

- **5.** Computational Thinker. Students develop and employ strategies for understanding and solving problems in ways that leverage the power of technological methods to develop and test solutions.

- **5b.** Students collect data or identify relevant data sets, use digital tools to analyze them, and represent data in various ways to facilitate problem-solving and decision-making.

CSTA K–12 Standards

ALGORITHMS AND PROGRAMMING

- **1B-AP-09.** Create programs that use variables to store and modify data.

- **2-AP-11.** Create clearly named variables that represent different data types and perform operations on their values.

- **3A-AP-14.** Use lists to simplify solutions, generalizing computational problems instead of repeatedly using simple variables.

K–12 Computer Science Framework

- **Practice 4.** Developing and using abstractions

- **Practice 5.** Creating computational artifacts

CCSS Mathematical Practices

- **MP.1.** Make sense of problems and persevere solving them.

- **CCSSM 2.OA.1.** Represent and solve problems involving addition and subtraction. Use addition and subtraction within 100 to solve one- and two-step word problems involving situations of adding to, taking from, putting together, taking apart, and comparing, with unknowns in all positions (e.g., by using drawings and equations with a symbol for the unknown number to represent the problem).

- **3.OA.8.** Solve problems involving the four operations, and identify and explain patterns in arithmetic. Solve two-step word problems using the four operations. Represent these problems using equations with a letter standing for the unknown quantity. Assess the reasonableness of answers using mental computation and estimation strategies, including rounding.

- **4.OA.3.** Use the four operations with whole numbers to solve problems. Solve multistep word problems posed with whole numbers and having whole-number answers using the four operations, including problems in which remainders must be interpreted. Represent these problems using equations with a letter standing for the unknown quantity. Assess the reasonableness of answers using mental computation and estimation strategies, including rounding.

Brennan and Resnick's Framework

- Being Incremental and Iterative.

Step-By-Step Instructions

For this project example, you will need to launch a new project from the MVS file menu and create a Console App using the C# language (see Figure 3.1). A console application is one designed to be used for a text-only interface program. Although MVS can be used to create graphical user interfaces, games, mobile apps, and web-based applications, the console application is typically used for beginning programming due to its simple and straightforward characteristics.

Give your new project a name (the example in Figure 3.2 is named "MyConsole-App") and note the location where your project will be saved.

Once the program loads, you will see the boilerplate template text shown below in the large window on the left side of your screen. This is the main editor where your programming code is entered, and it is where you will spend most of your time. The smaller Solution Explorer window to the right shows all of the files that are part of a project, which lets you launch other files to open in the main editor.

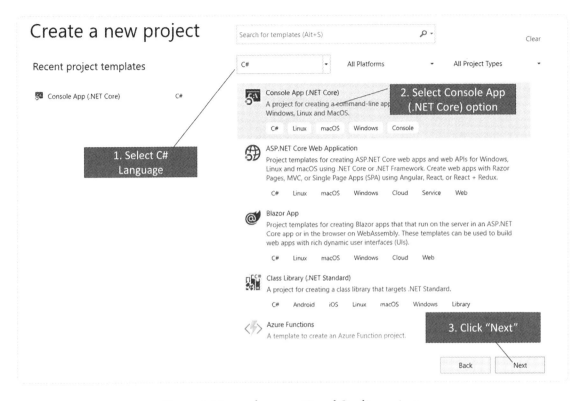

Figure 3.1 Launch a new Visual Studio project.

The window along the bottom of the screen (see Figure 3.3) is the output window and will be used for debugging. For now, we will concentrate on the main editor window. Notice the use of curly braces ("{ }") to create a hierarchy in the code. Each beginning brace must have an ending brace, and the editing window depicts gray dotted lines to indicate which braces are paired. The rightmost set of braces contains the Main method, which tells the computer where your program begins. Your Main method created from the template should have the "Console.WriteLine("Hello World!");" line in it already. But if you have an older version of MVS, you may need to enter this line yourself. If you need to enter it, make sure to end the statement with ";". All statements in the Main method must end with a semicolon.

The Console.WriteLine statement is actually a separate method that executes specific code on the information contained in the parentheses. In this case, it tells the computer to write the line of text in the quotation marks ("Hello World!") to the

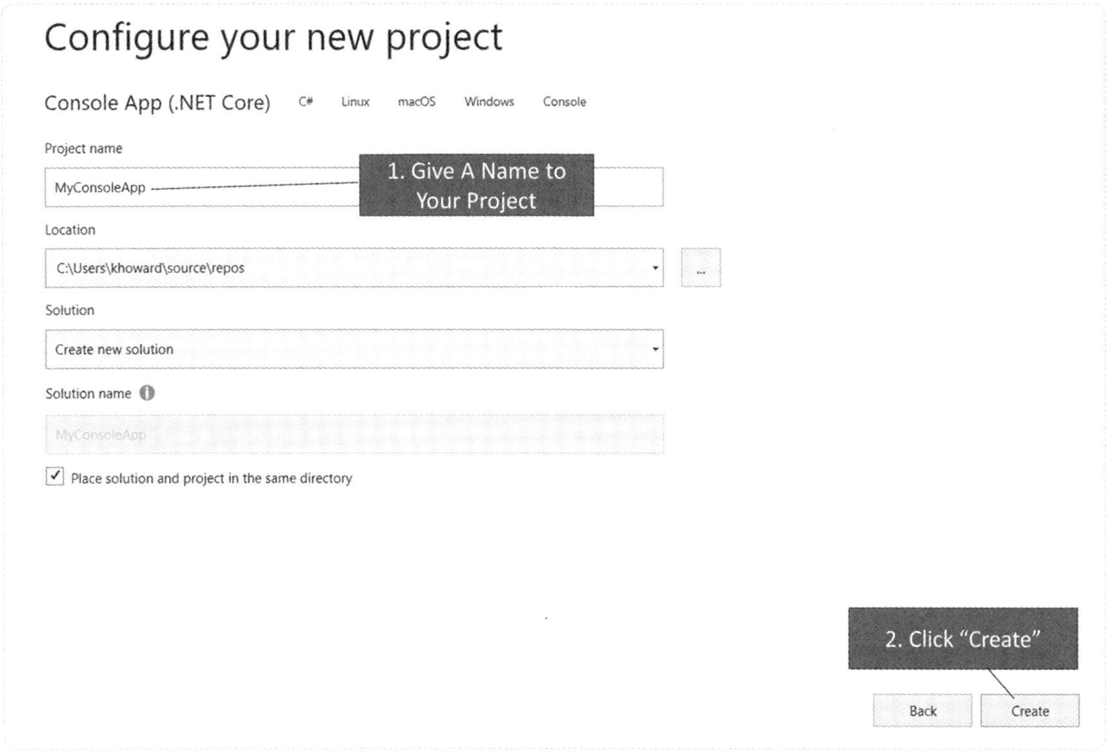

Figure 3.2 Name and create new project.

console application window. Although it's just a few lines of code, this represents a complete program that can be run across many types of computers to produce the same results that it does here. Have the students run the program by clicking on the green triangle on the icon bar above the main editor (see in Figure 3.3).

The output window displays the text contained in the Console.WriteLine statement (see Figure 3.4). While congratulations are in order for creating a program, the next step is to explore ways to add more functionality. According to Brennan and Resnick's Framework, this practice could be considered "Being Incremental and Iterative," whereby students apply an adaptive mindset as they test parts and play around with the code. Additionally, such an activity gives students an opportunity to strengthen their ability to "make sense of problems and persevere in solving them" (CCSS.Math. Practice.MP1).

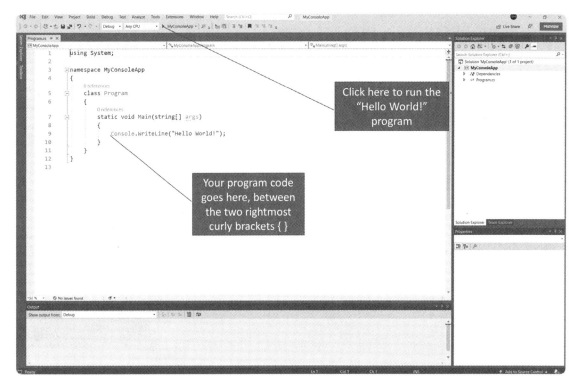

Figure 3.3 Project startup window containing *Hello World!* program boilerplate code.

One of the most important practices programmers will learn is commenting within their code. Comments help to narrate the action taking place in a program and provide insight into the thinking behind it. This will help the programmer, and others who read the code later, to understand what was intended when the code was written. Research has found that a programming learning approach requiring students to comment on their logic and intended structure before actually writing code improves the accuracy and proficiency of their coding (Sengupta, 2009). Unfortunately, due to the extra time it takes to provide thorough comments in code, even seasoned programmers don't always take the time to provide a solid roadmap for their programs.

The syntax used for writing comments in a programming environment varies across different languages, but in C# a line is rendered a comment when it starts with two forward slashes (//). This tells the computer that anything on the line after the

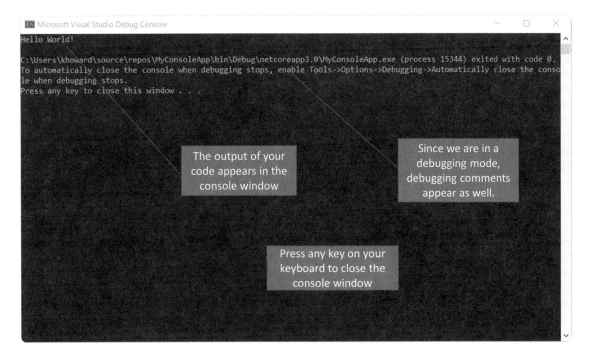

Figure 3.4 Hello World! program output.

slashes is commentary and should not be executed as code. Text across multiple lines can be commented either with a beginning "/*" and an ending "*/" or by using double forward slashes at the beginning of each line. To cultivate good programming habits, beginners should be encouraged to document their steps as much as possible. For the exercise illustrated below, students would be instructed to write a comment line to describe the text that they will be printing to the console, followed by a WriteLine() method with the to-be-printed text in quotes. They can simply edit the existing WriteLine statement to reflect their own statement. Remind students to end the statement with a semicolon and to make sure they don't remove any of the curly braces; otherwise, they will receive errors when they run the program. As before, they will click the run icon to start the program in a console window.

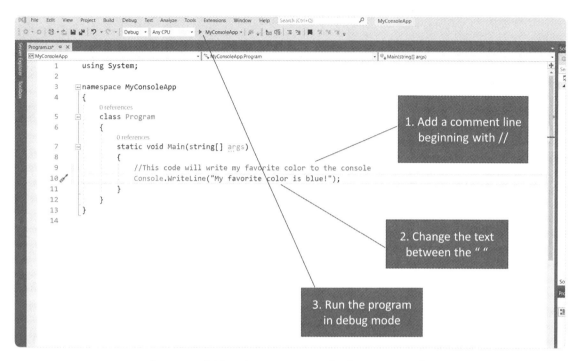

Figure 3.5 Add code comment and edit output code.

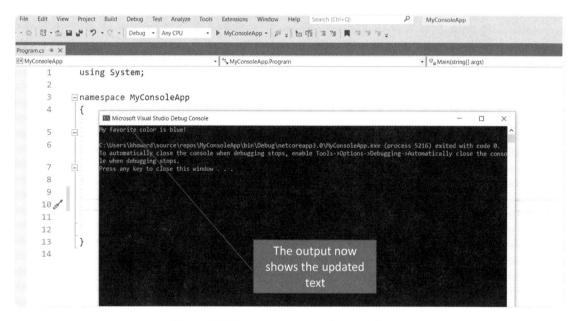

Figure 3.6 Program output after revisions.

The console app window now displays the students' revised text. As before, the console window can be closed by pressing any key on the keyboard. Next, we will change our options to clean up the debugging code that appears when we run our console application.

Under the Tools menu, select "Options" and then put a check next to the option shown in the graphic featured in Figure 3.7. Note that you may have to scroll to the bottom of the dialog box window to find the option. Click "OK" once you have checked the option.

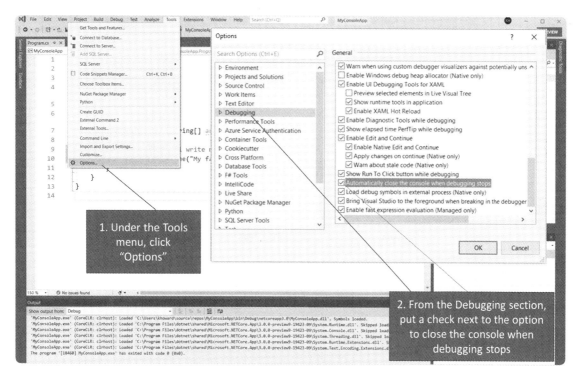

Figure 3.7 Changing project options.

If you run the program now, you will no longer see the debugging text. However, it may run and close so quickly that you will not have a chance to read your output. Therefore, you'll want to add one additional statement to your program (shown in Figure 3.8).

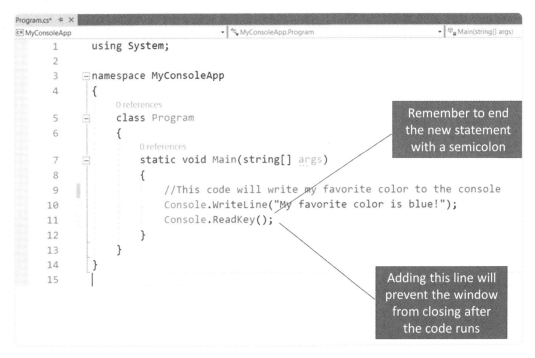

Figure 3.8 Adding *Console.ReadKey();* statement.

The additional statement will allow your program to run without the extra debugging text, and your output will be clean, containing only the information you programmed it to write (see Figure 3.9).

Figure 3.9 Program output after project option change.

Now let's move on to working with *variables*. We'll start out with the string type variable, which is used frequently in programming. As previously noted, string variables are used to hold data that will be identified and manipulated as text. Although a text variable can store numbers, it stores them as text as well. This means that you cannot perform calculations on any numbers stored in them (without first converting them), just as you cannot perform meaningful calculations on words or letters. To perform calculations, the data needs to be stored in a numeric variable such as an integer or float variable type. The next exercise will allow us to manipulate data stored in string variables and will highlight the kinds of issues that can arise when they are treated as numeric variables in most programming languages.

Have students update their console application code to read as shown in Figure 3.10. The code includes a comment for each line of text to explain what the programmer intends to happen. Experienced programmers usually do not comment on

```
3  namespace MyConsoleApp
4  {
       0 references
5      class Program
6      {
           0 references
7          static void Main(string[] args)
8          {
9              //This code will write my favorite color to the console
10             Console.WriteLine("My favorite color is blue!");
11
12             //ask user for their favorite color
13             Console.WriteLine("What is your favorite color?");
14
15             //get user's favorite color and store it to the string variable userFavColor
16             string userFavColor = Console.ReadLine();
17
18             //comment on the user's favorite color
19             Console.WriteLine("I think " + userFavColor + " is a nice color!");
20
21             //pause the program so that the user can read the output
22             Console.ReadKey();
23         }
24     }
25 }
```

Console.ReadLine() is used to read data provided by the user

The string variable holding the user input is used in the response

Figure 3.10 Completed project code.

each line of code; instead they comment on selected lines or entire blocks of code at a time. However, beginners can benefit from having to think through and explain their programming intentions and will find these explanations helpful when trying to pick up on a project days later. The code on line 10 has not changed (note that your line numbers may be different depending on your spacing). Line 13 asks the user what their favorite color is and stores their answer in a string variable named "userFavColor". A new command is introduced on line 16: Console.ReadLine(), which reads the user's response to the question and assigns it to the string userFavColor. Note that the string userFavColor is being declared and assigned the value from Console.ReadLine() in the same line.

Line 19 uses the data provided by the user (favorite color) as part of the sentence responding to the user. The user's favorite color is stored in the string variable userFavColor and is added to sentence text before and after it. Note the use of "+" signs when adding strings and/or string variables together. Also note that spaces need to be entered in the quote marks to keep the words from all running together when the strings are combined. A comment has been added above the Console.ReadKey() statement to explain its purpose. The output of the program is shown in Figure 3.11.

Figure 3.11 Program output from completed project.

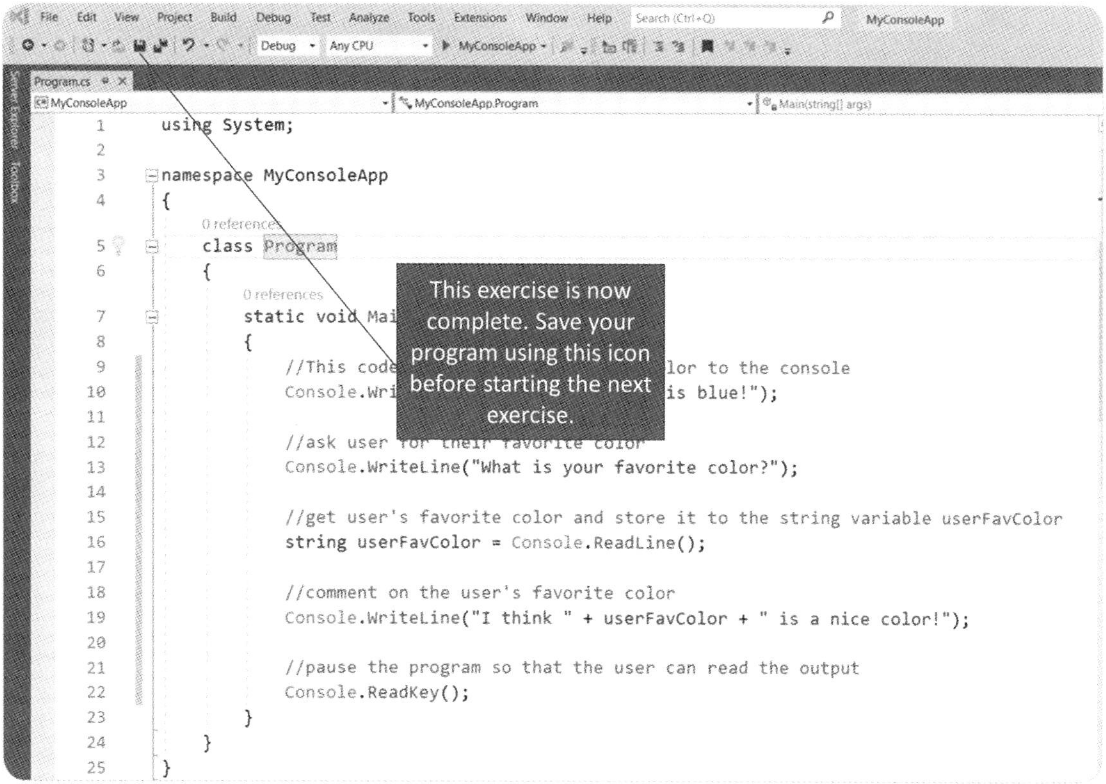

Figure 3.12 Saving the project.

Before moving on to the next exercise, save your program file as shown in Figure 3.12.

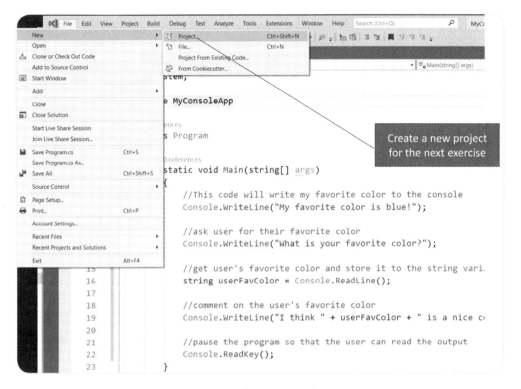

Figure 3.13 Start new project.

For the final exercise in this chapter, students explore declaring mathematical and Boolean variables. We'll start off with a new project using the menu option shown in Figure 3.13.

From the dialog window, select the C# language option and Console App, as before (see Figure 3.14).

Name the project "MyVariableApp" and create the project (see Figure 3.15).

The Console.WriteLine("Hello World!") line can be replaced with the MyVariable-App code (downloaded from the book website) to save time. However, if an instructor would like to provide students with practice coding from scratch and working in the MVS code editor, they can enter the code shown in Figure 3.16 manually.

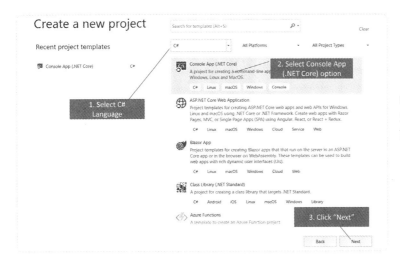

Figure 3.14
Select programming language and project type.

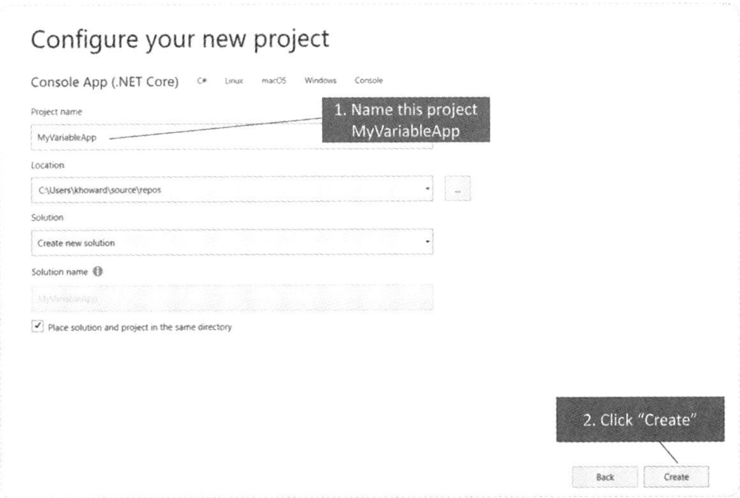

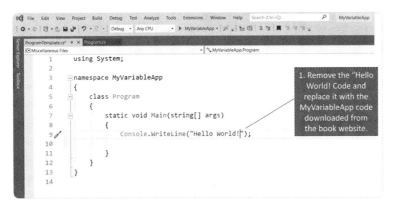

Figure 3.15
Name new project "MyVariableApp".

Figure 3.16
Replace Console. WriteLine("Hello World!") statement with project code shown in next figure (3.17).

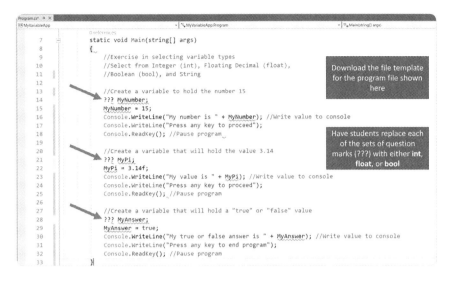

Figure 3.17
Type or download the code shown here from k12stemequity.com. Replace "???" with "int", "float", or "bool".

Figure 3.17 shows the program after the "Hello World!" statement has been replaced by the template text for this exercise. The code shown only needs to have the three variable declarations completed with the variable type required for the respective data descriptions. The arrows point to placeholder text (???) that needs to be replaced with either "int", "float", or "bool" based on the data requirements for each. You will notice wavy red lines below some of the text in the program similar to the spell-check functionality seen in many word processors and browsers. In this case, the warnings are part of an extensive code-checking function Microsoft calls

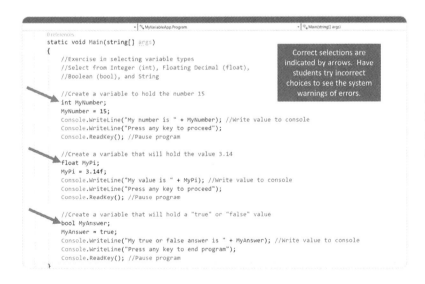

Figure 3.18
Project code with the correct variable types entered.

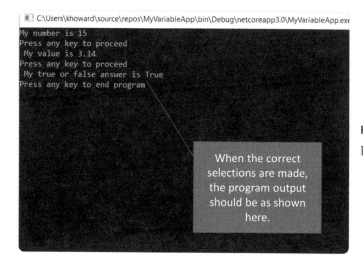

My number is 15
Press any key to proceed
My value is 3.14
Press any key to proceed
My true or false answer is True
Press any key to end program

When the correct selections are made, the program output should be as shown here.

Figure 3.19 Corrected program output.

"Intellisense," which alerts the programmer that some syntax needs to be corrected. Just as with word processors, the user can hover over the wavy red line to activate popup boxes that provide clues as to what needs to be corrected. The use of programming environments with functions such as these assists beginners in learning syntax and finding common errors before they get to the debugging stage.

In this case, the variables have warnings on them because they have not been properly declared in the program. Once students have been made aware of the different kinds of data that can be stored in each data type, selecting the correct answers should be pretty straightforward. However, it is helpful to encourage them to attempt to select incorrect data types to learn how the editor guides them to correct their mistakes.

Figure 3.18 displays the program completed with the correct variable types entered in place of the placeholders. Notice that once the correct answers were entered, all of the wavy red lines disappeared and the program runs without issues.

Figure 3.19 shows the output to the console window when the program is run. In each case, the program stored and wrote each of the variable values as expected.

Mathematical Connections

Although the program compiled to complete the console application project is a rather simple one in terms of functionality, it engages a number of math concepts that strengthens students' understanding of them. The discussion of variable types starts to form their understanding of the differences between integers and floating decimals, even if they are not yet ready to perform calculations. The assignment of data to a variable (albeit text data) starts to plant the idea of using a variable to represent something else, as well as using that variable as part of a larger process. Learning variable types should include discussing how the Integer type can be used to hold whole numbers. Common Core State Standards for Mathematics (CCSSM) call for students to be performing addition and subtraction operations with positive integers as early as kindergarten (K.CC, K.OA) and multiplication and division of positive integers by grade 3 (3.OA, 3.NBT). By grade 4 , they call for students to understand decimal notation for fractions (4.NF) and to perform operations with decimals to hundredths by grade 5 (5.NBT), both of which align with the Float variable type. Students are expected to determine whether equations involving addition and subtraction are true or false by grade 1 (1.OA), giving context to the Boolean data type. Given that these are concepts that students are expected to start grasping in K–5 classrooms, programming approaches that insulate students from the thought processes necessary to declare variables in code miss an opportunity to help shore up their foundation in some basic math and CS concepts.

Dr. Cory Gleasman shares his approach to preparing preservice teachers to use coding with their math instruction. He challenges the notion of putting too much focus on a specific tool or platform, warning of the potential developmental harm that can come from bringing the math content in as an afterthought to a coding lesson, rather than purposefully integrating it within. His insights inform elementary teacher education in CS and math pedagogy.

Coding + Math during Preservice Teacher Development

DR. CORY GLEASMAN

Assistant Professor of Computer Science Education at Tennessee Technological University

I've witnessed the lack of K–5 CS education provided by university teacher preparation programs. Not only are K–5 preservice teachers apprehensive of the terms *computer science* and *coding*, but so are teacher educators who are preparing our future teachers. Computer science and coding are not the same and are frequently mistaken for one another, especially by preservice teacher candidates. Computer science consists of broad overarching theories of computing. While coding is a skillful act contingent upon the understanding of CT concepts and computing knowledge bases, when instructing elementary preservice teachers I have found explaining this differentiation to be imperative for them to be successful with instruction on lesson plans involving block-based coding. For the past four years, I have been researching the cross sections of K–5 mathematics and block-based coding languages in order to offer preservice teachers a practical approach to integrating CS into their instruction. Furthermore, I have set out to establish a set of design guidelines for teacher educators to follow if they wish to create a higher-education learning environment, enabling K–5 preservice teachers to integrate coding into their mathematics instruction. I have placed an emphasis on viewing the cross section between K–5 mathematics and coding through a computational thinking lens and then using the intersection of computational thinking to create math teaching opportunities.

Through multiple instructional and research study iterations, I developed a five-week intervention course called Block-Based Coding and Computational Thinking for Conceptual Mathematics (B2C3Math). It was created to serve as a template for integrating block-based coding into elementary preservice teacher mathematics methods courses. The feedback surrounding the implementation of this intervention course has been extremely positive. The B2C3Math intervention was implemented three times at the University of Georgia and is currently in its fourth iteration at Tennessee Technological University.

The notion of using coding as a tool to facilitate mathematics is not new. In the 1980s,
Seymour Papert detailed his coding-mathematics learning theories in his memorable
book *Mindstorms: Children, Computers, and
Powerful Ideas*, and they are still relevant
today. What is different is the plethora
of tools and accompanying frameworks
at our disposal. Many times it becomes
overwhelming having so many coding
platforms as options, and a focus is placed
on the tool and the products made from
manipulating the tool. Within B2C3Math,
preservice teachers are taught to ensure
learning opportunities are occurring during
the coding process and not dependent
upon a coded product. I preach that coding
platforms can and will forever change;
however, the underlying concepts can be
engaged to elicit similar mathematics learning regardless of the technologies in play. The
focus on the overlapping of math and coding
concepts in the form of CT helps promote the
learning of both math and coding, not just the

Block-Based Programming

Computational Thinking

Elementary Mathematics

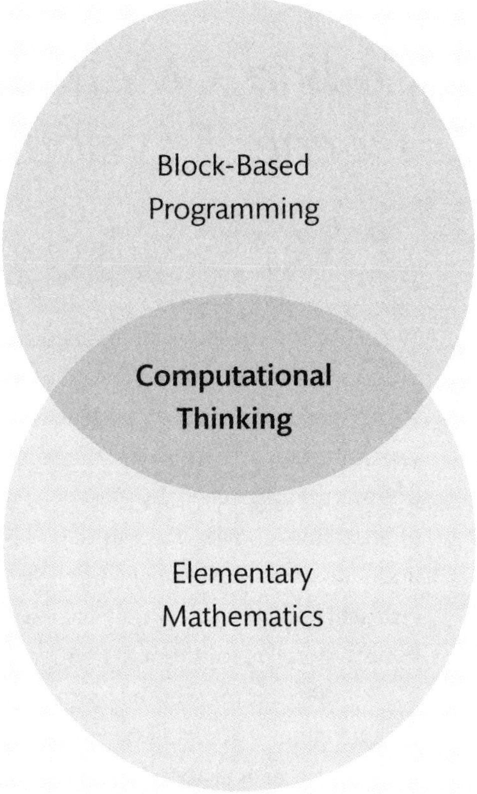

Figure 3.20 Cross section between mathematics and coding (photo credit: Gleasman & Kim, 2018).

procedural learning of a block-based coding language. I witness preservice teachers
rely on drag-and-drop coding curriculums, which are time-efficient, but can be more
harmful than good, especially at the developmental level. Helping preservice teachers
understand how to develop a coding-mathematics activity has been more beneficial
than teaching a mapped-out coding curriculum during teacher preparation. During
the first B2C3Math iteration, preservice teachers tended to plan a lesson where their
future students were coding; however, math learning followed the coding process and
was dependent upon visual outputs. Design guidelines and instruction associated with

B2C3Math were altered to ensure preservice teachers evoked math learning to occur simultaneously with coding processes.

Much data and relevant findings have surfaced as a result of research surrounding B2C3Math, but the most impactful and eye-opening conclusion I realize after its implementation is preservice teachers enjoy the innovation and creativity required to create coding-math lesson plans. They have expressed that coding and CT are an avenue in which to teach elementary math. While participating in the B2C3Math course, many preservice teachers were hesitant to develop coding lesson plans; however, I have witnessed preservice teachers alter their attitudes and perceptions. They now view the incorporation of block-based coding-math lessons as a feasible way to enhance their future students' mathematical understanding.

For more information regarding the B2C3Math intervention, see our article in Springer's *Digital Experiences in Mathematics Education Journal* titled "Pre-Service Teachers' Use of Block-Based Programming and Computational Thinking to Teach Elementary Mathematics" (Gleasman & Kim, 2020).

 # Mission Clarity

Working with data is a fundamental expectation at the core of computer programming. Number sense, as the foundation upon which mathematics is built, is foundational to students' deep understanding of all branches of mathematics. Likewise, data sense is at the heart of programming. Understanding how to manipulate different forms of data is crucial to becoming a good programmer. Understanding how to declare, initiate, manipulate, read, write, and store data takes purposeful effort.

If programming in K–5 education is viewed as primarily a means of self-expression with just a *side order* of CT, then the effort it takes to understand the fundamentals of programming may seem too steep to be entirely necessary. Conversely, if the long view of preparing students for secondary education, and ultimately for potential careers in information technology, is taken, then it is imperative that we familiarize students with the most basic of concepts that comprise CS. Whichever purpose an educator pursues in this regard, we encourage them to make students and parents partners in the decision-making process. Not every student aspires to have a career as a computer programmer one day, nor is every student longing for tinkering and self-expression through digital channels. Thus, a one-size-fits-all model of CS is not likely to best serve all students. Building a CS program around just one approach is a surefire way to ensure that some students' wants and needs will be excluded.

RESOURCES

RESOURCE	SOURCE	LINK	
C# Data Types Reference	Tutorials Point		(iste.org/standards/computational-thinking)
Java Data Types Reference	Tutorials Point		(tutorialspoint.com/Data-types-in-Java)
C# Reference for Built-in Data Types	Microsoft Corporation		(docs.microsoft.com/en-us/dotnet/csharp/language-reference/keywords/built-in-types-table)
Visual Studio Download	Microsoft Corporation		(visualstudio.microsoft.com/downloads)

CHAPTER 4

Operators and Loops

This chapter explains how math operators are used in CS and what similarities and differences exist between the two disciplines. The chapter also explores
loops and how they function in programming.

Included in this chapter:

- Project using the tool Flowgorithm to create loops
- Comparison of loop function across programs
- Resources for deeper exploration of operators and loops

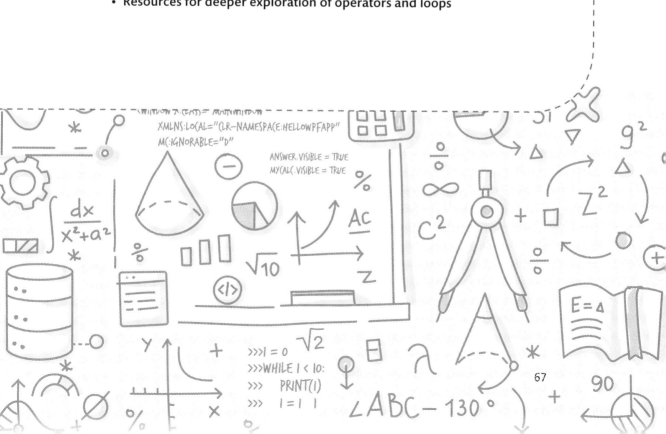

Operators

Knowledge of basic math operators transfers effectively to a programming environment due to the fact that their use in coding mirrors their frequent use in math learning. Addition and subtraction use the same symbols (+, –) and operate for the most part just as they do in standard math exercises. Multiplication and division use different symbols than students may be used to (* and / rather than x and ÷, respectively), but otherwise operate the same as students have become accustomed to using them. Likewise, relational operators (e.g., <, >, =, >=, <=) appear and behave exactly as they do in elementary math textbooks and commonly encountered exercises. Students can build confidence in their programming skills while strengthening their math proficiency by programming tasks that utilize these skills in solving problems or executing tasks that require them. This can provide relevance to skills that are sometimes learned in isolation, which can enhance students' motivation to increase math proficiency as well.

The use of the equals sign (=) can cause some confusion for the novice programmer, as it is interpreted differently in code. In math, $a = 4$ means the two are equal, as in a is already equal to 4. In programming, the equals sign (=) is an *assignment operator* rather than part of an existing equation. In programming, $a = 4$ is interpreted as "let $a = 4$" and is used to assign values to variables. If I then wanted to change the value of variable a to 6 in a code statement, I could add to the current value of variable a by writing "$a = a + 2$", which simply adds 2 to the current value of a (4) to make it 6. Alternately, I could overwrite the old value by writing "$a = 6$" to set the new value. You may recall our previous C# variable declaration example "int MyCount = 5", which was used to declare the integer type variable "MyCount" and assign the value of 5 to that variable in one statement.

Loops

Loops are an important and powerful core programming concept that greatly enhances the efficiency with which programs can operate. It is common that a program will need to iterate through the same steps of a given process multiple times, and loops enable the programmer to ensure that the process occurs exactly the same way each time. It also makes program flow easier to understand for someone reading the code. The flowchart in Figure 4.1 depicts the anatomy of a programming *loop*. The flow starts at the *Program Entry Point* and proceeds to the *Condition* symbol, where a condition is tested to determine the next step. If the condition is true, the program enters the loop and executes the code contained in the *Body of Loop* symbol. Upon completing the "body" of the program code, the program loops around and returns to the Condition symbol to test it again. As long as the condition remains true, the program repeats the loop over and over again. Once the condition evaluates to false, the program exits the loop and proceeds to execute any code that follows the loop.

The Condition symbol in the loop represents a decision point, which is handled in code by Boolean logic. Boolean operators are used frequently in programming and can present problems to beginners. We previously noted that Boolean variables are binary variables that have only two possible values: true or false. In programming, this can be represented logically by "yes or no," numerically by "1 or 0," or in a Boolean logic statement that evaluates to true or false. The three primary operators in Boolean logic are "And", "Or", and "Not". The symbols can vary by programming language, but in C# (and some others) the symbols are as follows: And = "&&", Or = "||", and Not = "!". For example, if a is true and b is false, the statement "$a \, || \, b$" evaluates to true, "$a \, \&\& \, b$" evaluates to false, and the statement "$!(a \, \&\& \, b)$" evaluates to true.

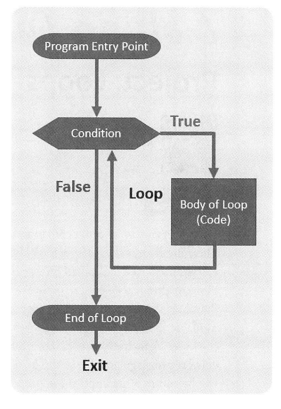

Figure 4.1 Flowchart of a While Loop.

Zhang and Nouri (2019) found that students using the Scratch block-based programming platform had difficulty in setting Boolean expressions and struggled with *nested loops* (a loop within a loop). They found low usage rates and varied levels of understanding of loops and indicated that students should be encouraged to include Boolean logic in their programs to enhance their comprehension of loops. The use of flowcharts can assist novice programmers in following the flow of a program through loop iterations, helping them to transition to abstract coding of repetitive processes.

Getting Out the Blocks
Project: Loops

 k12stemequity.com/loops

Overview

Flowcharts are an effective tool to model program flow for young programmers. There are many flowcharting tools, both free and commercial, but for this example we will use a free tool called Flowgorithm (downloadable from flowgorithm.org). Flowgorithm is a PC-based application that allows users to build programs using flowchart symbols and run the programs within the application. The program is available in thirty different languages and is accessible even to younger learners in the lower elementary grades. For older, more advanced learners, Flowgorithm can convert programs into C# code (or several other programming languages) so they can be run in other application program interfaces. We will create a loop program, and then, for more advanced learners, we'll export the code to Microsoft Visual Studio (MVS) and run the program in a console application.

Duration

Depending on your students' familiarity with Flowgorithm and MVS, they will need approximately forty-five minutes to an hour to complete this project. Allow students to work in pairs, when necessary, and give students time to discuss any obstacles or difficulties encountered while working through their projects.

Standards Addressed

CSTA/ISTE Standards for Educators

- **5b.** Cultivate a supportive classroom environment that values and amplifies multiple solutions, approaches, perspectives, and voices.

ISTE Standards for Students

- **5.** Computational Thinker.

- **5c.** Students break problems into component parts, extract key information, and develop descriptive models to understand complex systems or facilitate problem-solving.

- **5d.** Students understand how automation works and use algorithmic thinking to develop a sequence of steps to create and test automated solutions.

CSTA K–12 Standards

ALGORITHMS AND PROGRAMMING

- **1A-AP-10.** Develop programs with sequences and simple loops to express ideas or address a problem.

- **1A-AP-14.** Debug errors in an algorithm or program that includes sequences and simple loops.

- **2-AP-10.** Use flowcharts and/or pseudocode to address complex problems as algorithms.

K–12 CS Framework

- **Practice 4.** Developing and using abstraction.

- **Practice 6.** Testing and refining computational artifact.

CCSS Mathematical Practices

- **MP.2.** Reason abstractly and quantitatively

- **MP.4.** Model with mathematics

CCSSM

- **K.CC.3.** Write numbers from 0 to 20. Represent a number of objects with a written numeral 0–20 (with 0 representing a count of no objects).

- **1.OA.8.** Work with addition and subtraction equations. Determine the unknown whole number in an addition and subtraction equation.

- **3.OA.9.** Solve problems involving the four operations and identify and explain patterns in arithmetic. Identify arithmetic patterns.

- **4.OA.5.** Generate and analyze patterns. Generate a number or shape pattern that follows a given rule. Identify apparent features of the pattern that were not explicit in the rule itself.

• **5.OA.3.** Analyze patterns and relationships. Generate two numerical patterns using two given rules. Identify apparent relationships between corresponding terms.

Brennan and Resnick's Framework

• Abstracting and Modularizing.

Step-By-Step Instructions --

Flowgorithm programs start with a Main symbol and an End symbol with a flow arrow connecting them, representing the beginning and end of your program (see Figure 4.2).

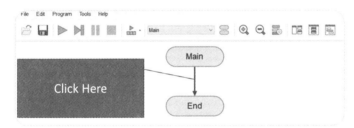

Figure 4.2
Flowgorithm startup window.

Double-clicking the flow arrow between the symbols will activate a popup menu shown in Figure 4.3.

Figure 4.3
Accessing popup menu.

72

Select the *Comment* symbol to enter your first program comment (Figure 4.4).

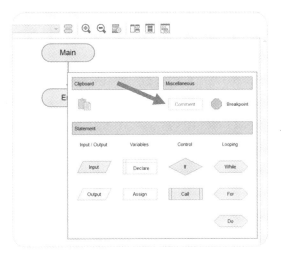

Figure 4.4
Adding comment symbol.

Double-click on the Comment symbol and add the comment as shown in Figure 4.5.

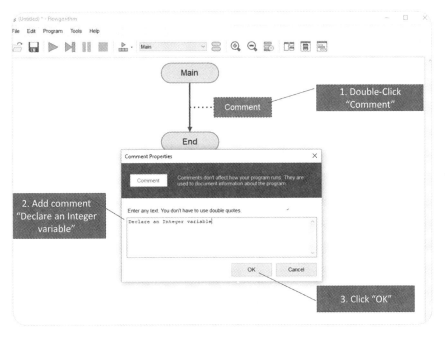

Figure 4.5
Adding comment.

Double-click the area of the flow arrow where you would like your next symbol to be inserted (see Figure 4.6). Insert the Declare symbol.

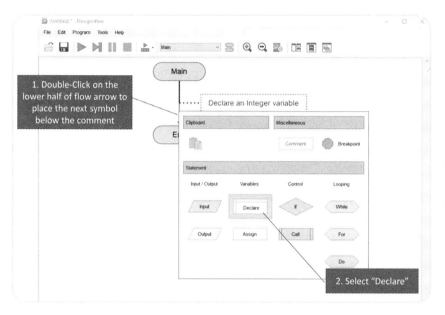

Figure 4.6 Access popup menu.

Enter the name of your Integer variable as "*x*" as shown in Figure 4.7.

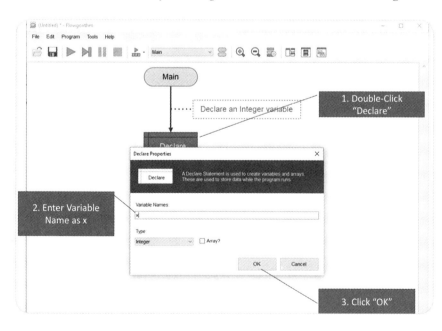

Figure 4.7 Enter variable name and type.

Next, we will assign 1 as the starting value of *x*. Double-click below the Integer declaration and select the Assign symbol as shown in Figure 4.8.

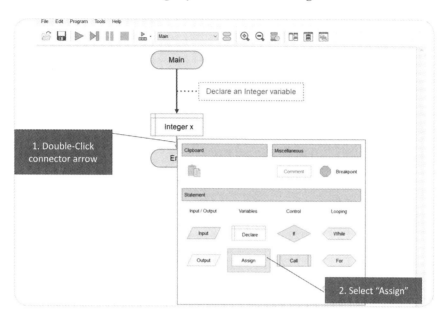

Figure 4.8
Access popup menu.

Now assign integer variable *x* a value of 1 as shown in Figure 4.9.

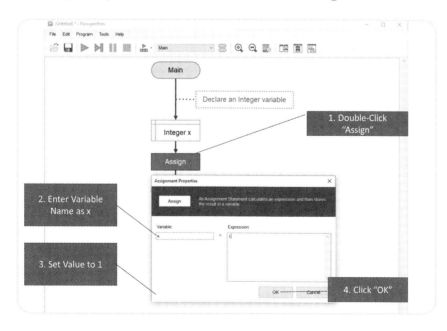

Figure 4.9
Set variable *x* value to 1.

Click the connector arrow below the variable assignment symbol and add a "While" loop symbol as shown in Figure 4.10.

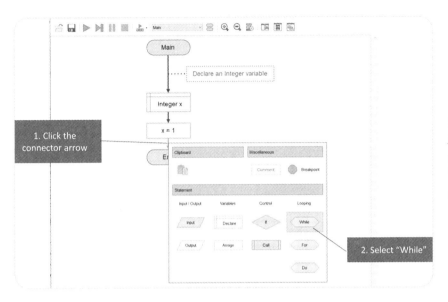

Figure 4.10
Access popup menu and select "While" loop symbol.

Click on the loop and add an Output symbol to it as shown in Figure 4.11.

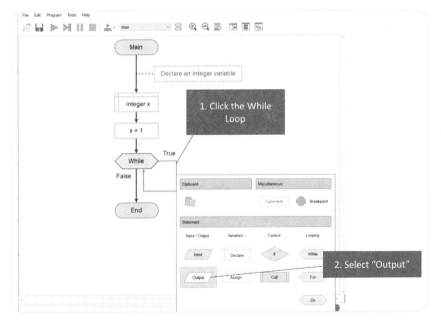

Figure 4.11
Access popup menu by clicking on loop and select Output.

Double-click the Output symbol and enter *x* into the expression box (Figure 4.12). This is telling the program that the loop is to print the current value of *x* to the screen.

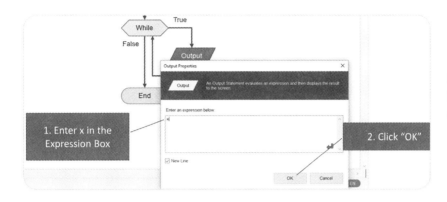

Figure 4.12
Set Output expression.

We need to set the condition under which the loop will continue to run. Double-click the While symbol to access its properties. In the popup window, set the *While* expression to "*x*<11". This means that the loop will continue to repeat until *x* reaches 11, at which time the condition will evaluate to False and the program will exit the loop.

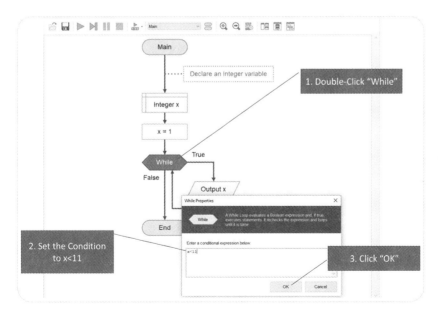

Figure 4.13
Set the "While" loop condition.

Next, click on the loop below the Output symbol and insert an assignment symbol. We will use this to increase the value of *x* by 1 each time the loop is run.

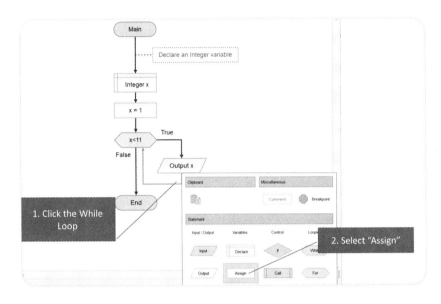

Figure 4.14
Access popup menu and select Assign symbol.

Double-click the Assign symbol and create the expression "*x* = *x*+1" to increase *x* by 1 each time the loop is executed.

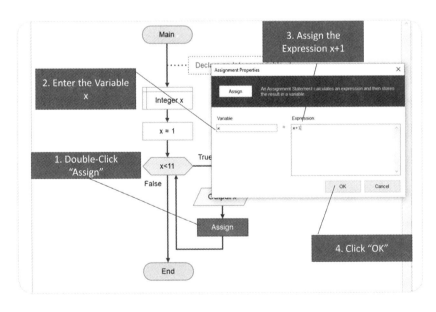

Figure 4.15
Assign expression.

Your completed program should look like Figure 4.16. Now it's time to run the program to see if the output is what we expect it to be. Click the green triangle on the menu bar to start the program.

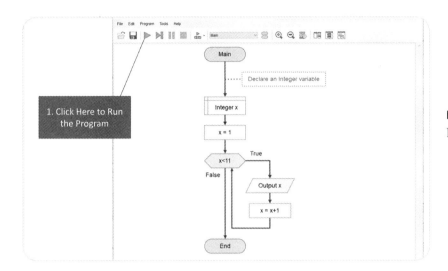

Figure 4.16
Run program.

The program executed as expected, cycling through the loop ten times and sending the value of *x* to the output window each time the loop was executed (see Figure 4.17).

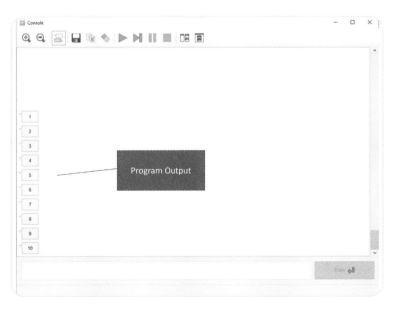

Figure 4.17
Program output.

From the main Flowgorithm window, you can launch the Source Code Viewer (Figure 4.18) to see what this program looks like in programming code language.

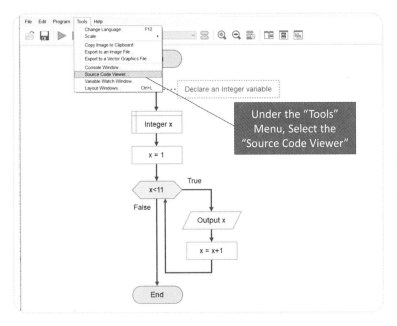

Figure 4.18
Open Source
Code Viewer.

The program can be viewed in the source code of several different programming languages as shown in Figure 4.19.

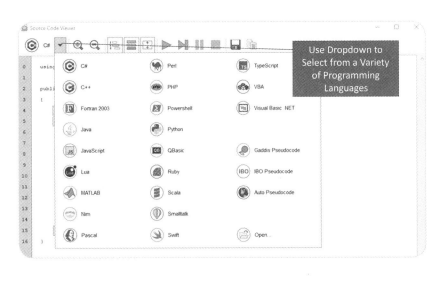

Figure 4.19
Select C#
coding
language.

Figure 4.20 displays the C# source code, which we will copy and paste into Microsoft Visual Studio. You have the option of using the source code in the development tool of your choice.

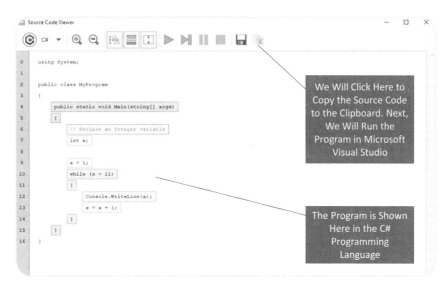

Figure 4.20
C# code syntax for program.

Open a new project in Microsoft Visual Studio using the C# language and Console App (.NET Core), just as we did in chapter 3 (see Figure 3.3). Name your project "MyLoop". Your editing window should look like Figure 4.21 with only the boilerplate "Hello World!" program in the main window. Delete everything in the editing window and paste the text you copied from Flowgorithm in its place.

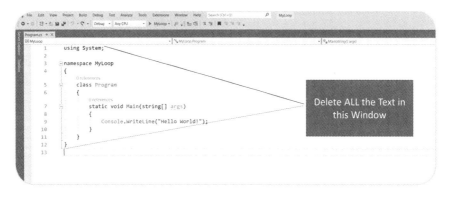

Figure 4.21
Delete code from new project code editor.

Your program should now look like the one shown in Figure 4.22, with the C# code copied from the Flowgorithm program. We will need to add the "Console.Read-Key()" line at the end of the program so that it does not close the console window before we have a chance to view the output. Make sure to place the cursor precisely where indicated on the figure before pressing the return key.

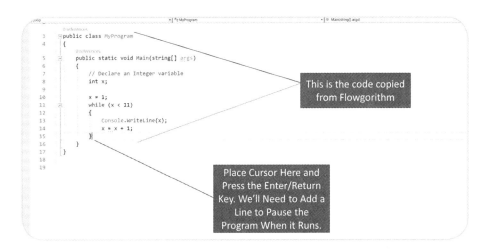

Figure 4.22 Paste code copied from Flowgorithm. Place cursor in code editor as shown.

Enter the code "Console.ReadKey();" shown on line 16 (see Figure 4.23). Once this line has been added, you should be able to run the program by clicking the green triangle in the menu bar.

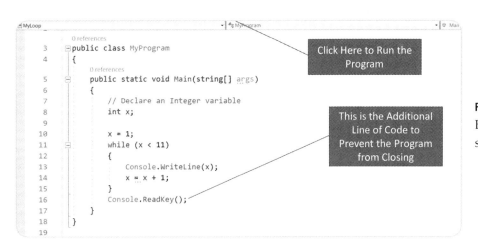

Figure 4.23 Enter ReadKey statement.

The console window displays the output (shown in Figure 4.24), which executed as expected.

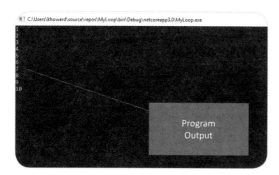

Figure 4.24
Program
output.

Mathematical Connections

Several math concepts were addressed by this project, providing opportunities to strengthen students' grasp of them through their programming efforts. The assignment of value to the integer variable revisits the CCSSM standards for kindergarten (K.CC, K.OA) and grade 3 (3.OA, 3.NBT) of working with integers. The assignment of a one-unit increment to the variable within the context of the While Loop ($x = x + 1$) addresses the grade 1 standard of working with addition and subtraction equations (1.OA). However, the mathematical hub of this exercise is situated in the condition statement for the programming loop. Understanding how to use Boolean operators and Boolean logic to evaluate condition statements as true or false directly assesses the grade 1 standard of determining whether equations involving addition and subtraction are true (1.OA.7).

Mission Clarity

This chapter has illustrated the use of loops, which are a core concept of programming across programming languages. They harness the ever-increasing power of computers to accomplish tasks far more efficiently. Programmers need to understand loops not only as a concept, but within the contexts that they will be expected to use them. Figure 4.25 depicts the same loop program in four different potential learning contexts, each with a different level of detail and abstractness. While each approach differs in level of complexity, none appear to be beyond the reach of some students along the K–5 continuum of learning. Although students will differ on their readiness for one option over another, it is important that they are not limited by a lack of choices to pursue levels of complexity commensurate with their abilities.

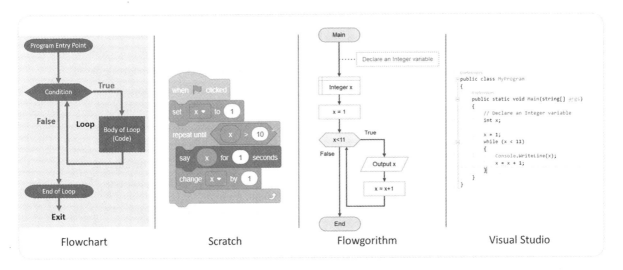

Figure 4.25 Comparison of While Loop program across different tools.

RESOURCES

RESOURCE	SOURCE	LINK
Flowgorithm Flowcharting Program	Sacramento State University	(flowgorithm.org)
Online Flowchart Designer	JGraph Ltd.	(draw.io)
SmartDraw (Online Flowchart Maker)	SmartDraw Software, LLC	(smartdraw.com/flowchart/flowchart-maker.htm)
Coding: Loops Vocabulary Activity	Flocabulary	(flocabulary.com/lesson/coding-for-loops)
Using While Lloops	Khan Academy	(http://bit.ly/3cMKD8z)

Events and Conditionals

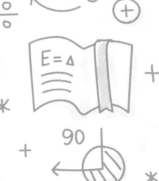

This chapter looks at events and conditionals as they operate in programming and offers advice on teaching them to students.

Also included in this chapter:

- Events and conditionals project using Microsoft Virtual Studio
- Student Voice feature: "Kamau's Coding Journey" written by a fourth grade student
- Resources for further understanding of events and conditionals

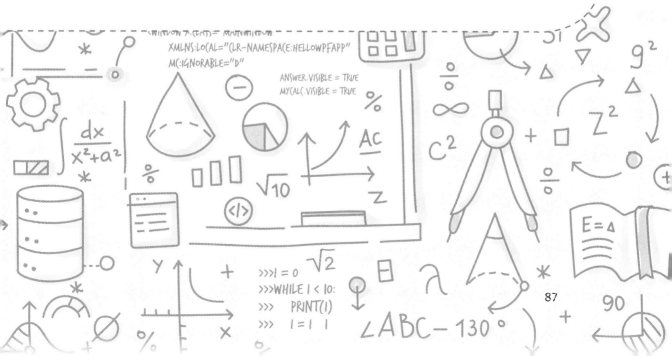

This chapter looks at two main components of programming, events and conditionals. Understanding how they are used to produce a particular outcome is important for students' understanding and development of coding and math skills.

Events

Events are the levers of action and responsiveness in computer and mobile apps, websites, and even robotics. The interactive nature of computers depends on code written to respond to events in a planned and purposeful manner. In productivity applications, events allow the program to respond appropriately to buttons and checkboxes, as well as to instruct the computer what to do with data entered in a text field. On mobile devices, the notification banners, badges, and sounds are responses to events triggered in code on the device. Computer games are wholly dependent upon events that trigger score and animated responses to actions by the user; event-driven programming is used extensively in applications with graphical user interfaces. Zhang and Nouri's (2019) review found that Scratch users, by and large, utilized events in the vast majority of their projects—particularly in the more recent studies cited. They did note, however, that students did not demonstrate sufficient use of complicated events beyond the "flag clicked event" often used to start a program or a "key pressed event". Given the extensive use of events in programming the kinds of interactive experiences computer users have come to expect, it is important for beginning programmers to gain a good understanding of how they work.

Conditionals

Conditional statements are at the heart of the decision-making processes that programs must navigate. We covered one type of conditional statement, the While Loop, in the previous chapter, but its decision-making was limited to whether or not to continue repeating the same block of code. Many programming decisions require that a choice be made between several different options based on multiple conditions. In more complex decision trees, more powerful conditional statements are required. The most commonly used decision-making statement is the "if" statement (also referred to as an "if-then" statement). They are often called to respond to an event, and their structure is such that certain blocks of code are only executed under the condition that a Boolean expression evaluates to true.

Table 5.1   **Conditional If Structure Examples**

EXAMPLE 1 *if*	EXAMPLE 2 *if - else*	EXAMPLE 3 *If - else-if - else*	EXAMPLE 4 *If - else-ifs - else*

If (condition)
{
   run some code ...
}
	If (condition)
	{
	   run some code ...
	}
	
	Else
	{
	   run different code ...
	}
		If (condition 1)
		{
		   run some code ...
		}
		
		Else if (condition 2)
		{
		   run different code ...
		}
		
		Else
		{
		   run different code ...
		}
			If (condition 1)
			{
			   run some code ...
			}
			
			Else if (condition 2)
			{
			   run different code ...
			}
			
			Else if (condition 3)
			{
			   run different code ...
			}
			
			Else
			{
			   run different code ...
			}

Table 5.1 depicts four examples of what the structure of if statements can look like in code. Example one is the simplest of the if statements, and it would only run the code between the curly braces if the condition evaluated to true; otherwise, the program would just continue to the next code below it. Example two runs the code below the if statement if the condition is true, but runs the code below the else statement if the condition is false. In example three, if condition one is true, the program will run the code under the if statement; if not, it will test for condition two, and if true, it will run the code under the else-if statement. If neither condition one nor condition two are true, it will run the code under else. Note that one and only one of the code blocks will be executed. Finally, example four adds multiple else-if statements and operates the same way as the previous example, as only one of the four code blocks will be executed. You can string together as many else-if statements as you like, each with its own condition.

Learning how to use these statements, particularly in the context of programming toward a particular outcome, goes a long way in developing students' ability to sequence and to apply logic to scenarios with predictable outcome options. Math learning is strengthened when the Boolean statements used in the conditions are based upon mathematical equations being evaluated as true or false. With this approach, the math is no longer arbitrary (as it may sometimes seem in common math exercises), but is essential to achieving a specific programming goal. Given the accepted and expected process of debugging that is part of the programming culture, learners can test their answers by running their program without any evaluation-based affect involved. This is a more self-regulated form of learning that can pay dividends across other subjects as well.

Getting Out the Blocks

Project: Events and Conditionals

k12stemequity.com/events-and-conditionals

To provide contextual examples of how events and conditionals are used in practice, we'll return to the Microsoft Visual Studio (MVS) development platform, but this time we will create a Windows Form-Based application, which is well-suited for demonstrating event-driven programming.

Standards Addressed

CSTA/ISTE Standards for Educators

- **5a.** Facilitate inquiry for student learning. Use inquiry-based learning to enhance student understanding of CS content.

ISTE Standards for Students

- **5.** Computational Thinker.

- **5d.** Students understand how automation works and use algorithmic thinking to develop a sequence of steps to create and test automated solutions.

CSTA K–12 Standards

ALGORITHMS AND PROGRAMMING

- **1B-AP-10.** Create programs that include sequences, events, loops, and conditionals.

- **2-AP-12.** Design and iteratively develop programs that combine structures, including nested loops and compound conditionals.

K–12 CS Framework

- **Practice 4.** Developing and using abstraction.

- **Practice 6.** Testing and refining computational artifacts.

CCSS Mathematical Practices

- **MP.2.** Reason abstractly and quantitatively.

- **MP.4.** Model with mathematics.

CCSSM

- **1.OA.7.** Work with addition and subtraction equations. Understand the meaning of the equal sign and determine if equations involving addition and subtraction are true or false.

- **3.OA.1.** Represent and solve problems involving multiplication and division. Interpret products of whole numbers, (e.g., interpret 5 × 7 as the total number of objects in 5 groups of 7 objects each).

- **5.OA.1.** Write and interpret numerical expressions. Use parentheses, brackets, or braces in numerical expressions, and evaluate expressions with these symbols.

- **5.OA.2.** Write and interpret numerical expressions. Write simple expressions that record calculations with numbers, and interpret numerical expressions without evaluating them.

Brennan and Resnick's Framework

- Debugging and Testing.

Step-By-Step Instructions

From a new project launch, select the Windows Forms App (.NET Framework) template to start (see Figure 5.1). For our example we have named the project "MyFormApp", but you can have students add their own name to the project name to add personalization (i.e., "MikesFormApp"). We have included selected screenshots in this chapter, but the full project instructions are available on the book website at K12stemequity.com.

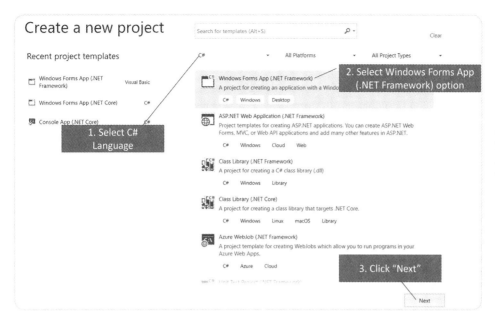

Figure 5.1
Launch new
project.

This student project requires that they write a math checker application that will check multiplication answers and provide feedback to the user. The completed application will include the use of a Windows form familiar to desktop applications, with textbox controls, labels, and a button. It will provide an introduction to object-oriented programming in that each of the controls is considered an object and has its own code procedures (called "Methods") dedicated to it. Objects have their own events as well, which are used to interact with the program user at runtime. Control objects are dragged to the form window and placed in the locations the programmer wants them to be at the time the application is run (see Figure 5.2).

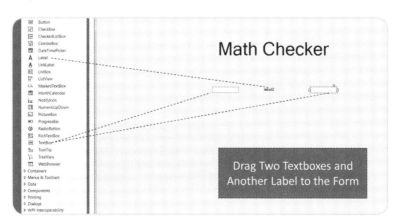

Figure 5.2
Drag and drop
controls on
form window.

This is not the same drag-and-drop concept as seen with block-based programs that drag actual syntax constructs (in the form of blocks that insulate the actual syntax) to the screen. These are objects that, while they have embedded code that governs their functionality, still require code behind them to make them work. These objects get their code instructions primarily from two sources. First, the embedded code or properties can be changed using the Properties window in the bottom-right corner of the screen. By changing these properties, we are able to alter the behavior and appearance of the objects from their default settings. The second way they get their instructions is through code we type in a code window—like we did previously for the console applications.

Figure 5.3 displays the completed form for our math checker application after the controls have been sized and arranged and their properties have been set as desired. Any object on the screen can be double-clicked to open the code window for the application so that we can code how events will be handled when the program is run. For this project, the user will enter three numbers (two numbers to be multiplied and the answer) into the textboxes on the screen. The user will then click the Check button to have the program check their answer and provide feedback as to its accuracy. Although this is a fairly short and simple program, it illustrates several of the concepts we have discussed thus far in this book.

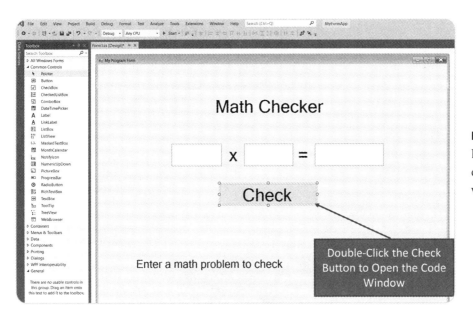

Figure 5.3
Launching the form code window from a window object.

For our project, we double-click the Check button to access the code window shown in Figure 5.4. Note that the code window and the form-design window are both still open. Select the tab for the window you wish to work on in the upper left corner of the editing window. Note that in the program code window, a method has been created to handle a click of "button1" (the default name assigned to the button on our form). All code placed in the curly braces of that method will be executed any time the button is clicked at runtime.

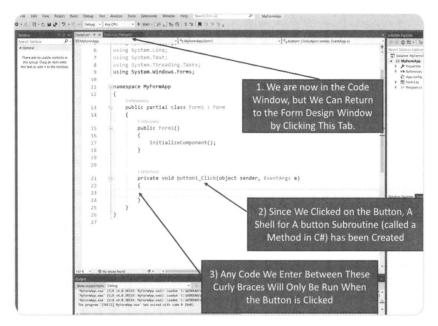

Figure 5.4
Project code window.

Figure 5.5 displays the code editor with all of the additional code needed to complete this project. (Note that comments were excluded to allow display of entire method.) The button-click event is the only one to which this program will be responding. Therefore, we do not need to put any code behind the other objects. We will discuss each of the sections of code in succession, starting with the variable declarations in the rectangle outline shown on Figure 5.5. The first line of code in the rectangle outline (line 27 of the code editor) is the declaration of a Boolean variable (bool) we have named "allboxesused". As its name suggests, this variable will be used to determine whether or not our user has entered a number in each of the three textboxes before clicking the Check button. You will recall that Boolean variables have one of two values: "True" or "False". The next line of code (line 28) is the declaration of three integer (int) variables that will be used to hold the numbers that the user puts into the textboxes. Each of these is initialized to a value of 0.

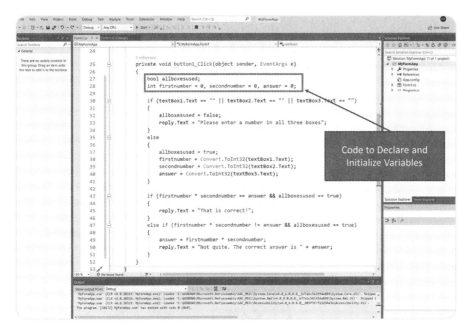

Figure 5.5
Variable
declarations.

Figure 5.6 outlines the second section of the event code, which is an if-else conditional statement used to confirm that the user is submitting valid data for the program to consider. The condition is the Boolean statement that essentially asks whether any of the input textboxes are empty. Note that the names of the textboxes are default values given by MVS when they were dragged onto the form (textBox1, textBox2, and textBox3), but we could have changed them to anything we wanted, as long as we followed the MVS naming conventions. The extension on each reference (e.g., textBox1.Text) is how the properties shown and set in the properties window are accessed via code. In this instance, each of the text properties is being read simply to determine if there is anything in them. If there is nothing in a textbox, then its text property will be an empty string, hence the use of "" in each equation. The use of the double equal sign (==) is to distinguish the "equals" sign from the assignment operator (=), which would actually set a value rather than check it. Finally, you will recall that "||" is used to represent the Boolean operator "Or" in C# code. Therefore, the if statement asks if textbox1 is empty Or textbox2 is empty Or textbox3 is empty. If any box is empty, this statement will evaluate true. This would cause the first block of code following the if statement to be executed, which sets the Boolean "allboxesused" variable to false and asks the user to put a number in all of the boxes.

If all of the boxes have been used, the else block of code collects the text from the boxes and stores it in the integer variables that we declared (i.e., "firstnumber", "secondnumber", and "answer"). The Convert.ToInt32() method that encapsulates each of the values is necessary because of the strict variable typing of C#; the Text property of a textbox is a string and therefore is incompatible with an integer variable, unless it is first converted to an integer.

Figure 5.6
If-Else
conditional.

The final section of code in the button-click event method is an if-else-if conditional statement (Figure 5.7). The if condition statement uses the Boolean And operator (&&) and therefore is asking if two things are both true: 1) is the equation accurate (first number times the second number = the answer)?, and 2) were all input boxes used? If both are true, then the text in the bottom label is changed to "That is correct!" If not, the answer is computed and given to the user by changing the bottom label to reflect the correct answer. Note the use of the multiplication operator (*) in the two conditions and the use of the Not (!) operator in the else-if condition.

Finally, note that the Name property of the bottom label was set to "reply" to make it easier to understand in code than "label3".

Figure 5.7 If-Else if conditional.

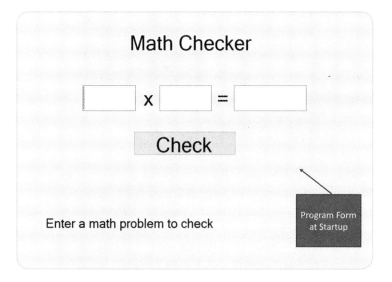

Figure 5.8 Program startup window.

Figure 5.8 shows the completed program at startup; Figure 5.9 depicts how the program responds when the user leaves one or more boxes empty; Figure 5.10 shows how the program responds to a wrong answer; and Figure 5.11 shows the correct answer response.

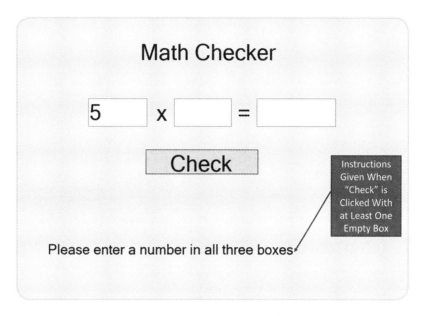

Figure 5.9 Program response to input error.

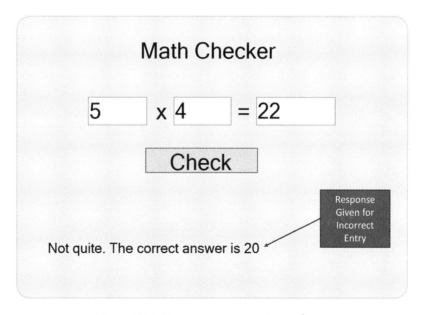

Figure 5.10 Program response to math error.

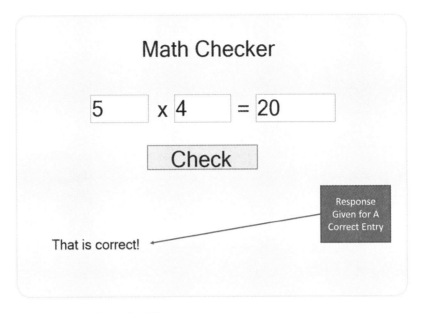

Figure 5.11 Program response to correct entry.

Mathematical Connections

This project provided reinforcement of the mathematical concepts addressed in the prior two chapters, as well as programmatic use of the Boolean operators (&&, ||, !) in the condition statements (1.OA.7). The Math Checker application required representing and solving multiplication problems, addressing the grade 3 Operations and Algebraic Thinking Common Core Standard (CCSSM 3.OA.1). It also addresses the grade 5 standards for writing and interpreting numerical expressions (5.OA.1, 5.OA.2).

Student Voice: Kamau's Coding Journey

KAMAU   Nine-Year-Old Fourth-Grader and Budding Computer Scientist

My first time coding was in an online camp where I learned Scratch coding. I started out by getting information about each block from the coding coach. Then I began making simple games, which ended up turning into masterpieces. I entered this program because it helped me a lot with block coding. I thought this was a good start for my coding journey. Next was Visual Studio. Instead of teaching me block coding, it taught me real code. I took my first step into Visual Basic. With my father assisting me, I made my first line of code: *Hello World*. After many more lines of code, I was finally making progress. Now I was making buttons, drop-down arrows, and so on. I finally made my first creation when I was able to write code with very little help. This, however, would need teamwork. My first build was a drop-down arrow that asked what your favorite restaurant was. I also made a calculator while I was in the program.

To get better at block coding, I did a school program called Code.org. It had many different online classes that I could take, and now I had no instructor to guide me. I was free. This, in my opinion, would be great for even teaching masters. There was one problem though. I was so focused on block coding I wasn't at all paying attention to actual JavaScript. This was a problem I could not ignore. Then an idea came to me. I knew I had a *Python for Kids* book in my room, and it had all kinds of code in it. So one day, I asked my parents if I could learn it. My mom entered the website, and I was taught plenty of JavaScript. The best part was that I was on my own for both block and JavaScript coding. Python allowed me to go from making simple math problems to creating lists that you could change in only a few words! The math problems were like "John = 100 and Bob = 200, then John + Bob = 300". After learning about the basics, I started learning to draw with *Turtles*. I did this program because I could finally do JavaScript without help. I thought this was a very good program for me to dabble in and have some fun.

Now I will state what I liked and didn't like about each program. Scratch coding is good in many ways. First, it has many categories, so navigation from one block to another is never difficult. Next, the blocks are easy to understand. Finally, you can take other people's published builds and carry them to your build using your backpack. The thing I don't like about this is that you can carry every block from someone's super-cool build and simply copy it. Another thing I don't like about Scratch is that the lessons can't be private, so you always have to have around three or four people with you, not including the instructor. At least you can be more interactive!

Next up is Visual Studio. I favored this program because it is not split screen. Yes, you have to switch between typing code and designing your workspace, but at least the words in the typing area are bigger! Another thing I noticed was that you can vary the size of buttons as well as name them. This is the same for some other stuff. What I don't like about Visual Studio is that the language is harder to understand.

The third program is Code.org. What I like about the program is that you get to complete big projects in no time. I also favor that you can either learn step-by-step, or make the code yourself. Finally, there are many different courses that you can take, so something fits for everyone. What I didn't like about Code.org was that it seemed like mostly games for small kids, but there was not that much actual coding.

The final program is Python. Python is a must-have because it allows you to learn JavaScript on your own. I also like Python because its language is easy to understand. The final thing that I favor about Python is that the book has a website too. What I don't like about Python is that the software doesn't run that well. Lastly, I don't like that you can't really do any code without the book and that you could lose the book and be in big trouble.

All in all, all of these languages have some pros and concerns, but they share one thing in common: they all helped me code.

 Mission Clarity

In this chapter, another core concept across programming languages was illustrated in an object-oriented programming (OOP) environment. Although much of the basic functionality of this program can be somewhat replicated in block coding platforms, Figure 5.12 illustrates how the two platforms are worlds apart in terms of usability and transferability outside of the programming environment. The Scratch program was able to collect and respond to the same user input using only one conditional statement—as opposed to two for the (OOP) version. The reason for this is that no data checking was required in the block-coding approach, as the program attempts to read your data and assign a type accordingly. As previously mentioned, this approach can lead to errors in text-based programming environments if the user is not adept at managing the use of variable types.

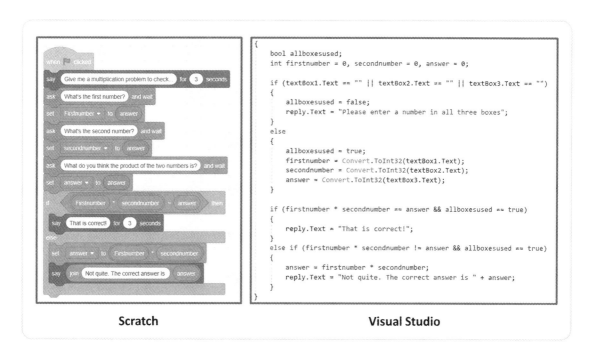

Figure 5.12 Comparison of if-else conditionals for Scratch and Visual Studio.

Conversely, in the OOP project, the student learns how to declare and set the variable type for Boolean and integer variables; use coding syntax for Boolean operators And, Or, and Not; set up both if-else and if-else-if conditional statements; convert incompatible data types for assignment to an integer; and assign object properties in code—none of which are accomplished in the block-based project. Perhaps none of these matters for students who have no interest in coding beyond its utility value in accomplishing the project task presented. However, for students who would gravitate toward the challenge and skills that the OOP project presents, it provides far more meaning to the work they are asked to do in their classroom. In either instance, students are called upon to reason abstractly and quantitatively (CCSS. Math.Practice.MP2) and to make sense of problems and persevere in solving them (CCSS.Math.Practice.MP1).

RESOURCES

RESOURCE	SOURCE	LINK	
Math Connections to Conditionals	MathGoodies.com		(mathgoodies.com/lessons/vol9/conditional)
How to Explain OOP to a Six-Year-Old	FreeCodeCamp.org		(http://bit.ly/2W11JtA)
C# Fundamentals Videos for Beginners	Bob Tabor Developer University		(http://bit.ly/2TV2r99)
Understanding Event-Driven Programming	Microsoft		(http://bit.ly/333kDlb)

RESOURCE	SOURCE	LINK	
Coding: Conditionals Vocabulary Activity	Flocabulary		(flocabulary.com/unit/ coding-conditionals)
Coding: Events	Flocabulary		(flocabulary.com/unit/ coding-events)
Conditionals with If, Else, and Booleans	Khan Academy		(http://bit.ly/2IAPID8)
Picademy (Raspberry Pi Professional Development)	Raspberry Pi		(raspberrypi.org/training/ picademy)
Python for Kids	Tynker Coding for Kids		(tynker.com/javascript)

CHAPTER 6

Diving Deeper into CS and Math Connections

This chapter shares research findings around math and CS and discusses how to teach reasoning and problem-solving through computer science.

Included in this chapter:

- Comparison of math performance and learning habits among math students

- Feature examining coding as a motivating factor for learning math.

- Coding project: "Native Peoples Bead-Looming Project Using Snap!" by Shana V. White

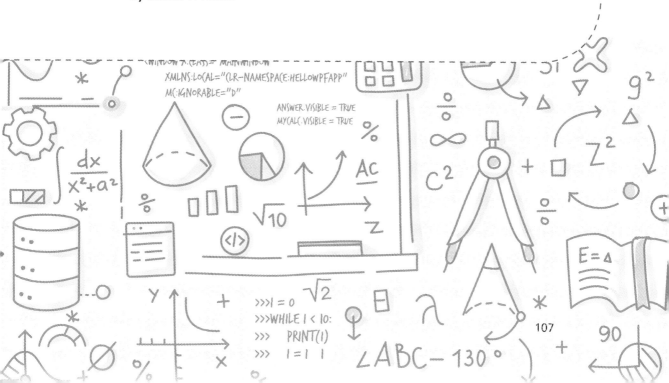

U sing CS to support strengthening math skills maximizes instructional efficiency and offers K–5 students opportunities to learn programming and
computing in meaningful ways. The National Assessment of Educational Progress
(NAEP) measured the progress of fourth-and eighth-graders: 2015 scores in math
decreased for lower-performing students and showed no significant change for
middle-and higher-performing students (NCES, 2017; Figure 6.1). Scores were
still higher than those first recorded in 1990; however, the fact that there were no
significant recent gains raises concerns about *what* needs to be done to support
achievement and for *whom*. One might assume that these data indicate math needs
to be taught more often and as a stand-alone subject, yet research on the influence
of math interest, and math identity on achievement, suggests that integrating CS
would raise levels of interest in math enough to support an increase in achievement.
In previous chapters, we offered case studies and research-based examples ("Getting Out the Blocks") for ensuring all students have access to opportunities that
foster self-expression and growth in math through the integration of CS instruction.

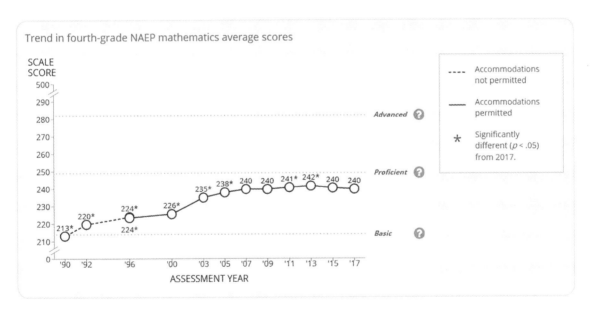

Figure 6.1 NAEP 2017 National Scores at a Glance.

As part of the NAEP assessments, students were also surveyed to offer insights into their experiences and achievements in math. In 2017, grade 4 students who indicated they worked in pairs or in small groups anywhere from once or twice a month to once or twice a week scored higher on average than their peers who collaborated less (or even more) frequently (Figure 6.2). The Organisation for Economic Co-operation and Development's Programme for International Student Assessment (OESD; PISA, 2009) administered a collaborative problem-solving assessment to thirty-two countries (and twenty partner countries and economies) to assess how well they collaborate with one another. Based on scores in math, science, and reading, students in Australia, Japan, Korea, New Zealand, and the U.S. performed better than expected on this assessment. What does this mean for teaching and learning CS in math for elementary students? Considering the demands of workplaces today, problem-solving in teams (or collaboration) is perhaps a skill in itself that can be learned through collaborative problem-solving. Leveling up and introducing paired-programming concepts to young learners may seem advanced; however, students commonly work with their elbow-partners in elementary classrooms already. Introducing these types of collaborative problem-solving opportunities in elementary classrooms prepares students early for working in teams, similar to how they may collaborate on future tasks in secondary classrooms or the workplace.

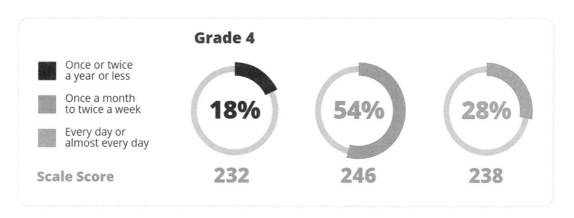

Figure 6.2 NAEP Report on Students Working in
Pairs or Small Groups to Talk about Math.

Currently, more than twenty-five states in the U.S. and the District of Columbia allow computer science courses to satisfy a math course requirement in secondary schools (NCTM, 2014). The conceptual overlap in these two content areas makes this possible. If CS courses can be utilized to satisfy math requirements at a secondary level, why not expose younger elementary students to CS through math instruction? More thoughts to consider are the potential instructional minutes saved when delivering integrated lessons, as well as the possible impact of the effective integration of CS on engagement and measured achievement for K–5 students, specifically in math. There are expectations from principals and districts when it comes to determining how instructional minutes are used in classrooms. Administrators want to hear more than "My students are engaged today," and districts want to see academic gains. "Math matters for computer science because it teaches students how to use abstract language, work with algorithms, self-analyze their computational thinking, and accurately model real-world solutions" (Sedlacek, 2016).

Promoting Reasoning and Problem-Solving

> Computational thinking is not thinking like a computer, as computers aren't capable of thought. Computational thinking describes a set of skills we can draw upon to solve a problem (Cross et al., 2016).

According to researchers, students often lack problem-solving and CT skills in the field of CS (Papadopoulous & Tegos, 2012). Without question, reasoning and problem solving-skills are critical in math. According to *Principles to Actions: Ensuring Mathematical Success for All*, "For students to learn math with understanding, they must have opportunities to engage on a regular basis with tasks that focus on reasoning and problem solving and make possible multiple entry points and varied solution strategies" (NCTM, 2014, p. 23). Reasoning and problem solving-skills are essential for students' success in math, basic coding, and CS in order to solve complex problems. When developing code to solve a problem, students are using both logical and abstract reasoning (Psycharis & Kallia, 2017). For example, if students were presented with a challenge to program a math game or work on a physical computing project, they would use CT skills to design before they code using a programming language such as Scratch or Snap! (See the "Getting Out the Blocks" section in this chapter). Students use their problem-solving skills to work out the algorithm for the game by decomposing the process into steps or rules that describe their game. Students will use abstract reasoning to help determine what information they should include in this process (CCSS.Math.Practice.MP2). Logical reasoning comes into play as the students make predictions in the programming process and analyze their final product.

The simple answer to the question of how to promote reasoning and problem-solving for your students would be to create opportunities for them to apply complex thinking skills. For example, teaching computer programming is one great way to promote higher-order thinking performance. Scholars even recommend adding strategies such as pair programming (Lewis, 2011) or anonymous peer assessments (Wang et al., 2016) to further promote critical thinking, reasoning, and problem-solving. Pair programming encourages a highly collaborative learning environment in which students support each other while going through programming procedures. Utilizing a peer assessment strategy gives students an opportunity to learn a project and then play the role of a reviewer from the teacher's point of view. Adding the element of anonymity to peer assessments can encourage students to think critically and perhaps offer more elaborate feedback on a peer's work than they may feel comfortable providing without anonymity (Gielen et al., 2010).

Educators such as Megan Brannon and Dr. Elena Novak share in the belief that it is important to promote the use of higher-order thinking skills through coding and math. As they share their perspectives in this chapter, they also highlight how developing coding language is similar to the development of language grammar skills, juxtaposing creative writing with innovative programming solutions.

Coding Success through Math Intervention

MEGAN BRANNON AND ELENA NOVAK, PhD

Learning to code offers many benefits. It helps students develop better problem-solving abilities and enhance their higher-order thinking skills (Falloon, 2016). In addition, coding engages students in genuine situations in which skills such as mathematics, algorithms, problem solving, and collective analysis can occur (Israel et al., 2015; Fessakis et al., 2013; Jona et al., 2014). The relationship between coding and math is not surprising, as coding, sometimes used interchangeably with computer science or programming, has its roots in mathematics. Byrne and Lyons (2001) discuss the relationship between math and coding, describing how the skills related to learning programming are comparable to the skills needed to be proficient in math. Additionally, coding skills assist students in becoming better mathematicians. A basic calculator can do arithmetic, just as most students can. However, to think mathematically, students need to understand how math functions authentically.

Research shows that coding can provide motivation for learning mathematical processes and skills (Calder, 2010). For example, in a study with the Scratch coding program, Calder (2010) found that while Scratch was not originally formed to facilitate the growth of math skills, the program clearly did immerse students in math concepts such as positionality, measurement (angle and time), and spatial perception. Calder (2010) also found that math skills were further developed using problem-solving, logic, and reasoning.

Nevertheless, learning to code is challenging for many students. Some of these challenges lie in the newness of the material, meaning the new syntax of the language (Ben-Ari, 2001). When learning to code, students learn new vocabulary, new concepts, a new programming language, and a whole new way of approaching the material. Malan and Leitner (2007) illustrate learning coding as learning a new language like Greek, with some pieces taken from the English language—but a wholly unfamiliar syntax. Byrne and Lyon (2001) also use a language comparison when they correlate language grammar skills to the syntax of a programming language, stating, "Attention to construction and syntax [in coding] might be considered similar to language grammar skills and creative writing skills might be considered similar to developing innovative programming solutions" (p. 52). Some foreign terms that students may have difficulty with include loops, variables, algorithms, Boolean expressions, and conditional logic (Malan & Leitner, 2007). These concepts are alien to most elementary students when they first learn coding.

Another issue with coding relates to the use of the technology. Technology is ubiquitous for students. Most students use devices often—both in and out of school. However, this does not mean that students are using their devices productively. Kafai and Burke (2013) describe our students—the digital natives—and explain that they may be able to use technology, but not always for purposes involving creativity, critical thinking, or productivity. Coding fits into both the critical- and creative-thinking categories.

Coding uses reasoning, logic, and inferential skills, which tend to be much more cognitively involved. According to Piaget, "Deductive reasoning is a cognitively advanced skill that develops during adolescence; in particular, adolescents acquire a complete mental logic that corresponds to standard logic" (Chao & Cheng, 2000, p. 40). Because deductive reasoning is not fully evolved until adolescence, many elementary students find it difficult to apply logic and reason to their study of coding. Students who code typically have to work through multi-step activities as well, which can be difficult for their short attention spans (Altun, Hazar, & Hazar, 2016). Keeping attention is imperative to success in the coding field, which sometimes requires time-intensive work to solve a problem. Math and coding can be viewed as two islands across from each other, close together yet not touching, and the concept of CT is the bridge between these two lands. Teaching both math and coding concomitantly helps to develop a strong mathematics *and* coding program.

Getting Out the Blocks

Project: Native Peoples Bead-Looming Project Using Snap!

BY SHANA V. WHITE

Overview

To provide contextual background, Shana's school is currently on Cherokee and Muscogee land in Gwinnett County. Native American bead looming is an important aspect of their culture. In this lesson, her students examined examples of bead looming and what stories the creations tell. They learned the importance of respecting the cultures of others and how other cultures are using math and computer science concepts in their customs.

Duration

Depending on your students' familiarity with basic coding concepts and Snap!, they will need approximately forty-five minutes to an hour to complete this project. Allow students to work in pairs when necessary.

Standards Addressed

CSTA/ISTE Standard for CS Educators

- **5c.** Promote student self-efficacy. Facilitate students' engagement in the learning process and encourage students to take leadership of their own learning by encouraging creativity and use of a variety of resources and problem-solving techniques.

- **5e.** Encourage student communication about computing. Create meaningful opportunities for students to discuss, read, and write about computing.

CSTA K–12 Standards
ALGORITHMS AND PROGRAMMING

- **1B-AP-10.** Create programs that include sequences, events, loops, and conditionals.

- **2-AP-12.** Design and iteratively develop programs that combine structures, including nested loops and compound conditionals.

K–12 Computer Science Framework

- **Practice 4.** Developing and using abstractions.

- **Practice 5.** Creating computational artifacts.

CCSS Mathematical Practices

- **MP.1.** Make sense of problems and persevere solving them.

CCSSM

- **3.OA.9.** Solve problems involving the four operations, and identify and explain patterns in arithmetic. Identify arithmetic patterns (including patterns in the addition table or multiplication table) and explain them using properties of operations.

- **4.OA.5.** Generate and analyze patterns. Generate a number or shape pattern that follows a given rule. Identify apparent features of the pattern that were not explicit in the rule itself.

- **5.OA.3.** Analyze patterns and relationships. Generate two numerical patterns using two given rules. Identify apparent relationships between corresponding terms.

Brennan and Resnick's Framework

- Being Incremental and Iterative.

Step-By-Step Instructions

Use a variety of beads and cords to design a bracelet that tells a story about confidence, perseverance, a source of pride, joy, resilience, overcoming obstacles, role models, or friendship.

Your bead pattern bracelet you create must tell this story about the aforementioned topics.

You and your partner will draw out your bead pattern on graph paper, noticing the coordinates and quadrants that your design will be in. You will also count the beads and cords you will need to create your project. You will need all of this information for the coding aspect of this project.

You must have all of the following ratios present in your bead design. It doesn't matter the colors you and your partner use, but these ratios (at a minimum) must be present. This must be noted on your graph.

(Ratio of 2:1)

(Ratio of 1:3)

You will write a narrative about your bead creation and design. Your narrative should be at least three paragraphs long and include examples of dialogue, figurative language, and strong word choice, and follow the plot structure of a short story. Try to zoom in into the memorable experience of how the bead design was created or why it is important to its people.

Finally, you and your partner will use Snap! to code your bead design digitally using the information from your graphing of the design earlier in the process as well as information from your teacher. (*Note for teachers:* consider preparing an example for students to further support their use of Snap!)

 Mission Clarity

Researchers also note the differences between programming platforms and how they may not all directly promote reasoning for young learners, but in some instances they do encourage "self-confidence in their problem solving ability" (Kalelioglu & Gulbahar, 2014, p. 33). In addition to the possibility of raising self-confidence, students typically enjoy the challenge that comes with programming (Siegle, 2009). That said, the tension between making curriculum decisions focused on self-expression, as opposed to CS preparation, has been addressed in previous chapters by acknowledging that the two can coexist. Furthermore, either path can serve to support strengthening math skills through CS, especially with the inclusion of CT as a bridge between the two.

RESOURCES

RESOURCE	SOURCE	LINK
Snap! Reference Site	University of California at Berkeley	(snap.berkeley.edu/index)
Sparking Student Creativity in Computer Science Makerspace	Learning.com Equip	(equip.learning.com)
Coding with Snap!	SAPEducation	(youtu.be/b-EWj7xN90U)
Introduction to Snap!	UC Berkeley and Education Development Center	(http://bit.ly/3aKwirJ)
Snap! (Programming Language)	Scratch Wiki	(http://bit.ly/2Q1tnD8)

Final Thoughts

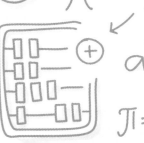

This chapter concludes with next steps for integrating computer science in your classroom or school and shares resources for professional learning networks and further learning.

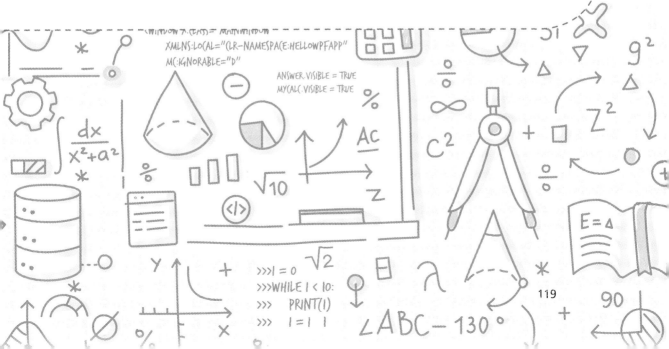

According to Grover and Pea (2013), there is little consensus about how to best prepare for changes that occur when implementing CS or the way CS should be included in K–5 instruction. Additionally, there are some researchers who contend that if CS is taught, the effective integration of CS occurs as a distinct discipline and a school subject in the K–12 curriculum (Angeli et al., 2016; Barr & Stephenson, 2011; Fluck et al., 2016). Despite debates and multiple perspectives about how K–5 educators prepare to teach CS, or if they teach it as a stand-alone subject, elementary teachers and students remain motivated and curious about CS-related content.

Now is the time to nurture students' curiosity for CS through the integration of coding and math, but don't stop at one hour of code. Consider moving beyond drag-and-drop! Drag-and-drop coding, also known as visual-based programming or block coding, has been used commonly during the Hour of Code initiative and as an introductory activity for students and teachers who are new to computer science. Students have used visual-based programming platforms, such as Scratch, to make a program or electronically construct details of computer coding by animating sprites. Text-based programming, such as Java, C#, and C++, includes lines of code to make a program.

Whether using visual-based or text-based programming, CS programs in K–5 include opportunities for students to code and create, develop problem-solving skills, learn programming concepts, and develop computational-thinking skills. Remember to seek "Mission Clarity" as you select the path for your students. The impetus for bringing in CS programs has been associated with the potential benefits for those who know how to program when entering the labor market (Moreno-León et al., 2016). Attention should also be given to the educational impact of learning to program from an early age, especially as it pertains to supporting the development of reasoning and problem-solving skills.

Similar to teaching other content areas, teaching CS requires educators to consider students' content knowledge to determine the appropriate lessons to facilitate. For example, if a unit using visual-based programming is introduced to the class and students seem to navigate the lessons with ease, their teacher may shift to text-based programming with more advanced concepts on a future assignment. The challenge can be that differentiating CS instruction requires additional content-knowledge preparation for teachers and planning time that is difficult to find when already developing instruction for several other content areas. Opportunities for K–5 educators to prepare for teaching CS are driven mostly by district initiatives or a teacher's personal desire to learn more about teaching CS in their classrooms (Howard, 2018). Yet K–5 educators are poised to push forward by leveraging their own curiosities in order to ensure all students have access to current CS opportunities.

 **Mission Clarity**

Next Steps

Attention must be given to the needs of K–5 educators who develop and deliver CS curricula, and we hope we have offered some support throughout this book. One lingering question may remain: what's next? If you are an administrator or campus leader seeking to implement a computer science program on your elementary campus, here are a few items to consider as you establish a sustainable implementation plan:

- Assess your school's technology hardware and software and fund necessary upgrades.

- Closely evaluate programs and solutions that only function on proprietary equipment and platforms that require costly professional development for continued use.

- Seek out open-source or freely available software-development platforms whenever possible.

- Assess the current CS knowledge of your teachers and edtech campus leaders.

- Determine the gaps in knowledge *with* your teachers, not *for* your teachers.

- Develop a plan to support your teachers with meeting their professional learning goals and encourage a focus on general (and transferrable) computing principles rather than a specific device or language.

- Identify and fund local and regional professional learning opportunities.

- Bring professional learning opportunities to your campus, such as a Teachers' Coding Club.

- Support and sponsor campus events that bring the entire community together to code.

If you are a K-5 educator, reading this book was one step in embracing the integration of CS in elementary. We hope that you continue to use the resources and tips offered throughout this book to help guide your CS instructional planning and content delivery. We also encourage you to seek out communities, such as those developed through the ISTE Computer Science Network, STEM Network, and CSTA organization (e.g., #CSK8) to stay connected to other educators and informed about relevant professional learning opportunities. Finally, visit k12stemequity.com for more resources and information connected to the thoughts and perspectives outlined in this book.

RESOURCES

RESOURCE	SOURCE	LINK	
ISTE Computer Science Network	International Society for Technology in Education		(http://bit.ly/38BgbLt)
CSTA	Computer Science Teachers Association		(csteachers.org/page/ join-csta)
Picademy (Raspberry Pi Professional Development)	Raspberry Pi		(raspberrypi.org/training/ picademy)
ScratchEd Community	ScratchEd		(scratched.gse.harvard.edu)
Codecademy	Codecademy		(codecademy.com)

RESOURCE	SOURCE	LINK	
CS Unplugged Teacher Resources	CS Unplugged		(classic.csunplugged.org/teachers)
Introduction to Programming in C#	Georgia State University–iTunes		(https://apple.co/2VWOASa)
CodeHero	Primer Labs Team		(codeherogame.wordpress.com/2016/09/04/codehero)
CSEdWeek	Computer Science Education Week		(csedweek.org/educate/hoc)

References

Altun, M., Hazar, M., & Hazar, Z. (2016). Investigation of the effects of brain teasers on attention spans of pre-school children. *International Journal of Environmental and Science Education, 11*(15), 8112-8119.

Angeli, C., Voogt, J., Fluck, A., Webb, M., Cox, M., Malyn-Smith, J., et al. (2016). A K-6 computational thinking curriculum framework: Implications for teacher knowledge. *Journal of Educational Technology & Society, 19*(3), 47-57.

Barr, V., & Stephenson, C. (2011). Bringing computational thinking to K-12: What is involved and what is the role of the computer science education community? *ACM Inroads, 2*(1), 48-54.

Ben-Ari, M. (2001). Constructivism in computer science education. *Journal of Computers in Mathematics and Science Teaching, 20*(1), 45-73.

Bers, M. U. (2018). *Coding as a playground: Programming and computational thinking in the early childhood classroom.* New York, NY: Routledge.

Blanton, M., Brizuela, B., Gardiner, A., Sawrey, K., & Newman-Owens, A. (2017). A progression in first-grade children's thinking about variable and variable notation in functional relationships. *Educational Studies in Mathematics, 95*(2), 181-202. doi:10.1007/s10649-016-9745-0

Brennan, K., & Resnick, M. (2012). *Using artifact-based interviews to study the development of computational thinking in interactive media design.* Paper presented at the American Educational Research Association, Vancouver, BC, Canada.

Byrne, P., & Lyons, G. (2001). The effect of student attributes on success in programming. *ACM SIGCSE bulletin, 33*(3), 49-52.

Calder, N. (2010). Using Scratch: an integrated problem-solving approach to mathematical thinking. *Australian Primary Mathematics Classroom, 15*(4), 9–14.

Chang, K.E., Wu, L.J., Weng, S.E., & Sung, Y.T. (2012). Embedding game-based problem-solving phase into problem-posing system for mathematics learning. *Computers & Education, 58*(2), 775–786.

Chao, S. J., & Cheng, P. W. (2000). The emergence of inferential rules: The use of pragmatic reasoning schemas by preschoolers. *Cognitive Development, 15*(1), 39–62.

Computer Science and Mathematics Graduation Requirements. (March 2015). Discussion paper for the board of directors developed by the Emerging Issues Committee of the National Council of Teachers of Mathematics.

Computer Science Teachers Association. (2017). CSTA K–12 Computer Science Standards, Revised 2017. Retrieved from http://www.csteachers.org/standards.

Cooper, S., Bookey, L., & GruenBaum, P. (2014). Future directions in computing education summit part one: Important computing education research questions. Technical Report CS-TR-14-0108-SC. Stanford: Stanford InfoLab.

Cross, A., Brothwick, A., Beswick, K., Board, J., & Chippindall, J. (2016). *Curious Learners in Primary Maths, Science, Computing, and DT.* London: Sage.

de la Pena, E. (July 17, 2017). *Visual-based vs. text-based programming.* Retrieved from: https://medium.com/@emily.f.delapena/visual-based-vs-text-based-programming-cb5438bc5405

Falloon, G. (2016). An analysis of young students' thinking when completing basic coding tasks using Scratch Jnr. on the iPad. *Journal of Computer Assisted Learning, 32*(6), 576-593.

Fessakis, G., Gouli, E., & Mavroudi, E. (2013). Problem solving by 5-6 years old kindergarten children in a computer programming environment: A case study. *Computers & Education*, 63, 87–97. doi:10.1016/2012.11.016

Fluck, A., Webb, M., Cox, M., Angeli, C., Malyn-Smith, J., Voogt, J., et al. (2016). Arguing for computer science in the school curriculum. *Journal of Educational Technology & Society, 19*(3), 38–46.

Gielen, S., Peeters, E., Dochy, F., Onghena, P., & Struyven, K. (2010). Improving the effectiveness of peer feedback for learning. *Learning and Instruction, 20*(4), 304–315.

Gleasman, C., & Kim, C. (2018). *Use of block-based coding in teaching conceptual mathematics.* Concurrent session at the Association for Educational Communications and Technology Conference. Kansas City, MO.

Gleasman, C., & Kim, C. (2020). Pre-service teacher's use of block-based programming to teach elementary mathematics. *Digital Experiences in Mathematics Education.* https://doi.org/10.1007/s40751-019-00056-1

Google & Gallup. (2015). *Searching for computer science: Accesses and barriers in U.S. K-12 education.* Retrieved from https://services.google.com/fh/files/misc/searching-for-computer-science_report.pdf

Grover, S., & Pea, R. (2013). Computational thinking in K12: A review of the state of the field. *Educational Researcher, 42*(1), 38–43.

Hammond, Z. (2014). *Culturally responsive teaching and the brain: promoting authentic engagement and rigor among culturally and linguistically diverse students.* Thousand Oaks, CA: Corwin, a Sage Publication.

Havard, D. D., & Howard, K. E. (2019). All advanced placement (AP) computer science is not created equal A comparison of AP computer science A and computer science principles. *Journal of Computer Science Integration, 2*(2), 1–19. https://org/10.26716/jcsi.2019.02.1.2

Howard, K. E., & Havard, D. D. (2019). Advanced placement (AP) computer science principles: Searching for equity in a two tiered solution to underrepresentation. *Journal of Computer Science Integration, 2*(1), 1–15. https://org/10.26716/jcsi.2019.02.1.1

Howard, N.R. (2018). EdTech leaders' beliefs: How are K-5 teachers supported with the integration of computer science in K-5 classrooms? *Technology, Knowledge and Learning,* 1–15. doi:10.1007/s10758-018-9371-2

Israel, M., Wherfel, Q. M., Pearson, J., Shehab, S., & Tapia, T. (2015). Empowering K-12 students with disabilities to learn computational thinking and computer programming. *Teaching Exceptional Children, 48*(1), 45–53.

Jona, K., Wilensky, U., Trouille, L., Horn, M., Orton, K., Weintrop, D., & Beheshti, E. (2014, January). *Embedding computational thinking in science, technology, engineering, and math (CT-STEM)*. Paper presented at the Future Directions in Computer Science Education Summit Meeting, Orlando, FL.

K–12 Computer Science Framework. (2016). Retrieved from http://www.k12cs.org

Kafai, Y. B., & Burke, Q. (2013). Computer programming goes back to school. *Phi Delta Kappan, 95*(1), 61–65.

Kalelioglu, F., & Gulbahar, Y. (2014). The effect of teaching programming via Scratch on problem solving skills: A discussion from learners' perspective. *Informatics in Education, 13*, 33–50.

Lewis, C. M. (2011). Is pair programming more effective than other forms of collaboration for young students? *Computer Science Education, 21*(2), 105–134.

Malan, D. J., & Leitner, H. H. (2007). Scratch for budding computer scientists. *ACM SIGCSE Bulletin, 39*(1), 223–227.

Mladenovi, M., Boljat, I., & Žanko, Ž. (2017). Comparing loops misconceptions in block-based and text-based programming languages at the K–12 level. *Education Information Technologies, 23*, 1483–1500. https://doi.org/10.1007/s10639-017-9673-3

Moreno-León, J., Robles, G., & Román-González, M. (2016). Code to learn: Where does it belong in the K–12 curriculum? *Journal of Information Technology Education: Research, 15*, 283–303.

Muro, M., Kulkarni, S., & Hart, D. M. (2016). America's advanced industries: New trends. *Brookings*. Retrieved from: https://www.brookings.edu/research/americas-advanced-industries-new-trends

Muro, M., Rothwell, J., Andes, S., Fikri, K., & Kulkarni, S. (2015). America's advanced industries: What they are, where they are, and why they matter. *Brookings*. Retrieved from: https://www.brookings.edu/research/americas-advanced-industries-what-they-are-where-they-are-and-why-they-matter/

National Center for Education Statistics. (2017). *The nation's report card: 2017 mathematics results*. Washington, DC: National Center for Education Statistics, Institute of Education Sciences, U.S. Dept. of Education.

National Governors Association Center for Best Practices & Council of Chief State School Officers. (2010). *Common core state standards for mathematics.* Washington, DC: Authors.

NCTM. (2014). *Principles to actions: Ensuring mathematical success for all.* Reston, VA: NCTM.

Organisation for Economic Co-operation and Development & Programme for International Student Assessment. (2012). *PISA 2009 technical report.* Paris: OECD.

Papert, S. (1980). *Mindstorms: children, computers, and powerful ideas.* New York, NY: Basic Books.

Papert, S. (1993). *Mindstorms: children, computers, and powerful ideas* (Second ed.). New York, NY: Basic Books.

Psycharis, S., & Kallia, M. (2017). The effects of computer programming on high school students' reasoning skills and mathematical self-efficacy and problem solving. *Instructional Science, 45*(5), 583–602.

Resnick, M., Maloney, J., Monroy-Hernandez, A., Rusk, N., Eastmond, E., Brennan, K., . . . Kafai, Y. (2009). Scratch: Programming for all. *Communications of the ACM, 52*(11), 60–67. doi:10.1145/1592761.1592779

Sedlacek, L. (2016). Math education: The roots of computer science. [Blog post] Retrieved from: https://www.edutopia.org/blog/math-education-roots-computer-science-lincoln-sedlacek

Sengupta, A. (2009). CFC (comment-first coding) – A simple yet effective method for teaching programming to information systems students. *Journal of Information Systems Education, 20*(4), 393–399.

Siegle, D. (2009). Developing student programming and problem-solving skills withVisual Basic. *Gifted Child Today, 32*(4), 24–29.

Stager, G. S. (2016). A heartfelt tribute to Seymour Papert. [Blog post]. Retrieved from http://childrenstech.com/blog/archives/17504

Tran, Y. (2018). Computer programming effects in elementary: Perceptions and career aspirations in STEM. *Technology, Knowledge and Learning*, (23), 273–299. doi: 10.1007/s10758-018-9358-z

Wang, X. M., Hwang, G. J., Liang, Z. Y., & Wang, H. Y. (2017). Enhancing students' computer programming performances, critical thinking awareness and attitudes towards programming: An online peer-assessment attempt. *Educational Technology & Society, 20*(4), 58–68.

Webb, H., & Rosson, M. B. (2013). *Using scaffolded examples to teach computational thinking concepts.* Paper presented at the proceeding of the 44th ACM technical symposium on computer science education. Colorado, US.

Whitaker, R. (2017). *The C# player's guide* (3rd ed.). San Bernardino, CA: Starbound Software.

Wing, J. M. (2006). Computational thinking. *Communications of the ACM, 49*(3), 33-35. doi:https://doi.org/10.1145/1118178.1118215

Wing, J. M. (2011). Research notebook: Computational thinking— What and why? Retrieved from https://www.cs.cmu.edu/link/research-notebook-computational-thinking-what-and-why

Zhang, L., & Nouri, J. (2019). A systematic review of learning computational thinking through Scratch in K-9. *Computers & Education, 141*, N.PAG-N.PAG. doi:10.1016/j.compedu.2

Index